D0436126

PANIC

PANIC

*The Betrayal of Capitalism
by Wall Street and Washington*

ANDREW REDLEAF
RICHARD VIGILANTE

RICHARD VIGILANTE BOOKS

PUBLISHED BY RICHARD VIGILANTE BOOKS
Copyright © 2010 by Andrew Redleaf and Richard Vigilante
All Rights Reserved
www.richardvigilantebooks.com
RVB with the portrayal of a Labrador retriever in profile is a trademark
of Richard Vigilante Books
Book design by Charles Bork
Library of Congress Control Number: 2009911906

Applicable BISAC Codes:
BUS027000 BUSINESS & ECONOMICS / Finance
BUS036000 BUSINESS & ECONOMICS / Investments & Securities

ISBN 978-0-9800763-6-3
0-9800763-6-6
PRINTED IN THE UNITED STATES OF AMERICA
10 9 8 7 6 5 4 3 2 1
First Edition

For Adam Smith, Frank Knight, and George Gilder

CONTENTS

PART I

By Purest Reason

CHAPTER ONE

The Anti-Entrepreneurs

Because the financial market crash of 2008, like the crash of 1929, followed a powerful prosperity it is often described as a crisis of capitalism, as if prosperity self-destructed. This is a primitive delusion, like believing drought and hailstorms are divine punishment on the inventors of crop rotation.

The crash of 2008 was driven by a betrayal of the most fundamental principles of capitalism, both in Washington and on Wall Street, by those often imagined to be capitalism's champions. This betrayal had little to do with the argument over whether government was too deeply, or not deeply enough, involved in the financial system. An unregulated financial sector is almost an oxymoron. In any modern state the government will always be the banks' biggest client and therefore will always make most of the rules, even if it pretends not to. The crash came not because we had too many regulators nor too few nor even because the regulators were incompetent. The crash came because both the regulators and the major players believed the same bad ideas.

The roots of the mortgage crisis, like the crash of 1987, the Long Term Capital crisis of 1998, and other market crises of our time are to be found in an ideology dominant in the financial establishment, on Wall Street and in Washington, through more than four decades. This ideology of modern finance replaces the capitalist's appreciation for *free markets* as a context for human creativity with the worship of *efficient markets* as substitutes for that creativity. The capitalist understands free markets as an arena for the contending judgments of free men. The ideologues of modern finance dreamed of efficient markets as a replacement for that judgment and almost as a replacement for the men. The most gloriously efficient of all, supposedly, were modern public securities markets in all their ethereal electronic glory. To these most perfect markets the priesthood of finance attributed powers of calculation and control far exceeding not only the abilities of any human participant in them but the fondest dreams of any Communist commissar pecking away at the next Five Year Plan.

Capitalism employs free markets as a proving ground, where the wise can be sorted from the fools, the good from the great. The ideology of modern finance calls only the market wise. As the Lord boasted to Gideon that he could make conquerors from cowards, the ideologues of modern finance offered to make any fool rich if only he renounced the first obligation of the capitalist, the burden of judgment.

The mortgage crisis and the crash of 2008 are sometimes described as problems of "liquidity": Too many of the nation's great financial institutions, we were told, lacked the cash to sustain their operations. Others say it was a crisis of insolvency, a fancy word for *broke*. Too many banks had invested in mortgages worth far less than the banks had paid. The banks were broke: they owed more than they owned.

These are half-truths. Like most grave financial crises, the mortgage crunch and the crash were crises of information. That's what panics are. Yes, the banks were short of cash but not because cash was scarce generally. The Federal Reserve and the world's other central banks had been pouring cash into the banking system for more than a year. Yes, some of the great banks were probably broke. But the real problem was not that some of the banks were broke but that at the critical moment none of them could prove they weren't.

The banks could not prove they weren't broke because under the influence of modern financial theory they had abandoned basic tools of analysis and judgment. For these they substituted elaborate, statistically based insurance schemes that, with the aid of efficient financial markets, were assumed to make old-fashioned credit analysis and human judgment irrelevant.

These schemes failed to make good judgment irrelevant. But they did make it impossible when it mattered most. It became impossible for either executives or regulators to fully understand the financial condition of any great modern bank. Balance sheets once amenable to due diligence became impossible to assess accurately not only in practice but almost in principle. Deprived of information, investors were deprived of judgment. They panicked, not for the first time in recent years.

A crisis of capitalism? Compare the repeated disasters in securities markets over the past few decades with the astounding success in the "real economy" during the same time. The Great Reagan–Clinton Boom was driven by an explosion of entrepreneurial creativity, touched off by two coincident trends. In the first trend, very large cuts in tax rates—starting with President Carter's substantial reduction of capital gains taxes—combined with the end of runaway inflation to increase after-tax returns on investment several times over, drawing capital out of hiding to seek out new ideas. Happily, new ideas were abundant. At the time of President Carter's first capital gains tax cut, the microprocessor was just seven years old.

The great boom was driven by inventors and investors whose good judgment connected suddenly abundant capital with suddenly abundant innovation. Relatively little of this connecting was done on Wall Street. The most important and innovative firms were launched far from public securities markets. What contribution there was from public markets often came from "wrong side of the tracks" neighborhoods like the junk bond market.

The men who launched the great boom were not gamblers. They did not make leaps in the dark. They brought light to the dark. They painstakingly turned hard-won knowledge into new wealth. Confronted with uncertainty they made their best judgments and then worked diligently to make those judgments come true. This process of confronting uncertainty and successfully resolving it usually by dint of hard work, diligent analysis, and sound judgment is the only source of what many economists have called "entrepreneurial profit" or sometimes "true profit." Entrepreneurial profit is the new wealth created after all the routine costs of business, not just labor and materials, but management and capital have been accounted for. Companies can go along for many years using the customary methods of their industry, making good money for workers, managers, and investors alike, without ever creating a true entrepreneurial profit. Entrepreneurial profit is what happens when a company suddenly turns fewer inputs into more outputs, lowers costs but increases revenues. Getting more out of less or something out of nothing is an act of creation (cf. "Let there be light"). In the economic sphere we call that act of creation entrepreneurship.

The great boom was driven by entrepreneurs: outsiders, upstarts, and innovators. The great mortgage meltdown was an establishment game. The mortgage-backed securities market was created and driven by the largest, most well-established, most heavily regulated and government-subsidized players in mainstream financial markets.

The new mortgage market and the novel financial instruments traded on it were also innovations, in a sense. They were certainly the result of an effort to make more appear out of less, perhaps even something out of nothing. But the Wall Street men were conjurers not creators. Throughout the years when they were constructing the machinery of disaster, Wall Street men were repeatedly praised for the "creativity" of their new lending devices. But theirs was not the creativity of the entrepreneur but the bureaucrat. Their avowed goal, their most cherished dream, was to isolate money management from flawed human judgment, including their own. As with bureaucrats everywhere, they craved the cover of rules and systems. Like the servant who hid his silver talent in the earth, fearing his master more than he trusted his own judgment, the bankers buried the capital confided to them in structure and schemes rather than accept the responsibility it implied.

The great boom was driven by the insights, diligence, and judgment of a relatively small group of entrepreneurs. Underpinning the ideology of modern finance is the notion that the insight, judgment, and even diligence of the entrepreneur are irrelevant for investing in public securities markets. These markets, we are told, are special, too powerful, and too perfect to allow any entrepreneur's judgment to matter.

Modern investment theory says that public securities markets—computerized, blazingly fast, effusively liquid—are as close as mankind has ever come to realizing the perfectly efficient market of classical economic theory. In such a perfect market, entrepreneurship is impossible. The entrepreneur's profit comes from superior judgment, but in a perfect market no one's judgment can be better than the market's. In the ideology of modern finance, attempting to exercise ordinary human judgment when building a portfolio of publicly traded securities is considered not only futile but actually dangerous. Judgment is everywhere to be replaced with structure and process. It is no accident that the various methods used to create the most complex mortgage-backed securities are comprised under the term "structured finance."

To say, as so many did in the wake of the crash, that the bankers were reckless, heedless of risk, is exactly the opposite of the truth. They were so obsessed with risk that they became terrified to live by their own judgment. If the ideology of modern finance had a motto, it might be "thinking doesn't work."

In the manner of ideologies, this one captured many who actually rejected its founding assumptions. The efficient market hypothesis—the notion that financial markets get prices more "right" than any investor can—is indispensable, logically, to modern investment theory. Yet by the time of the crash the efficient market hypothesis was far less widely accepted than it had been twenty years earlier. The tech wreck and other market catastrophes had left few money managers willing to swear their undying allegiance to the all-knowing market. Yet, even as specific notions underlying the reigning ideology were discredited, the ideology itself grew stronger. Ideologies are like that; it is part of their power. When a set of ideas becomes an ideology, the ideas can themselves all but disappear into the background, like air or gravity.

It was not bad theory alone that caused the crisis. A clutch of the top executives of our greatest banks joined with fly-by-night mortgage brokers and august agencies of the government in an unspoken conspiracy of fraud, with their own institutions among the ultimate victims. While the fraud was happening it was winked at and even encouraged by nearly every relevant regulatory and political authority, with a few ineffectual exceptions.

The ideology was essential to the deception, especially the self-deception. It gave cover to temptations that, had they appeared in their raw and rabid form, might have been resisted. Tempters everywhere seek the cover of respectability, and nothing was more respectable, more impeccable, even scientific and statistical, than the contemporary theory of investment. The bankers fervently believed their new structures and systems would better ensure the soundness of their loans than old-fashioned credit analysis and human judgment, fraught as ever with human error. Having crafted a system that seemed to relieve them of responsibility for making good judgments, they naturally proceeded to make an enormous number of bad loans. Similarly, the government did not know the banks' financial condition not because the banks were hiding it but because the banks themselves did not know. Believing that statistical systems could transcend the need for human judgment, the bankers created and the regulators encouraged financial institutions with balance sheets no one could judge.

Finally, when the fraud began to be revealed by its consequences, the government turned crisis into catastrophe. It was the government that actually collapsed stressed credit markets, largely by treating fraud as mere misfortune. Transfixed by the same ideology of irresponsibility, the government coddled those who perpetrated the fraud and concentrated its ire on those who exposed it, especially short sellers. (Short selling is to financial markets what free speech is to political markets.)

The ideology of modern finance tears capitalism in two, and then abandons the half beyond the ken of bureaucrats and the professors who train them. Capitalism demands free markets because it needs free minds. Modern investment theory says efficient markets can moot the minds entirely. The entrepreneur cherishes freedom including the freedom to fail. The bureaucrat of capital dreams of a world in which failure is impossible. Confronted with demons of uncertainty, the entrepreneur wrestles them till dawn. The bureaucrat of capital crafts idols of ignorance and worships in the dark.

Prevailing in Washington as on Wall Street were the most vile and self-destructive assumptions of anti-capitalists everywhere who imagined they could wield capital even while abandoning the principles that created it; that systems could substitute for the moral standards they once embodied; or that men who lost trillions of dollars of other people's money might somehow recover it if only the government would give them trillions more. Crony capitalists on the right and socialists on the left united as always behind their most fundamental belief, that wealth is to be captured by power and pull rather than created in the minds of men.

CHAPTER TWO

A More Perfect Market

" Here is a flat-out prediction for the New Year. Sometime in the next twelve to eighteen months there is going to be a panic in credit markets. Spreads,[1] which now hover at an extremely tight 300 basis points [3 percentage points] or so, will gap to more than 1,000 basis points. To put it another way, prices of high yield securities will drop by something like 20 percent with some weaker paper plunging even deeper."

So one of us, Andrew, predicted in December of 2006, thus forecasting in surprisingly (to us, anyway) accurate detail the great credit crunch that began in 2007 and culminated in the crash of September 2008. Curiously enough, Andy had also predicted the crash of 1987 almost twenty years before. Both predictions arose out of a diagnosis of a deep flaw in American financial markets and theory, a flaw that amounted to a betrayal of capitalism in the very places supposed to most perfectly exemplify it.

That December 2006 prediction of a crack-up in credit markets was made in Andy's monthly letter to clients of Whitebox Advisors. Andy, who founded Whitebox in 1999, is CEO. Richard is communications director. The letter, on which we work together every month, combines Andy's insights into current market opportunities and investment strategies with an ongoing conversation we have been having on economics and philosophy and what all else since we met in college in 1975.

In that December 2006 letter we went on to explain that "the driver in the credit market panic of 2007 or 2008 will be a sudden, profound, and pervasive loss of faith in the alchemy of structured finance as currently practiced."

What did we mean?

"Structured finance" is the practice of dividing up a large pool of investments, carrying a certain level of risk, into smaller pools, some of which will then have higher risks than the original pool (and carry bigger payments to investors) and some of which will have lower risks than the original pool (and carry lower payments to investors).

If that sounds impossibly abstract, consider this example, simplified, but more or less drawn from real life. All around the country mortgage "originators" (which may be banks but are more likely mortgage specialists like Countrywide or New Century) are making loans to homebuyers. These mortgages are rated for quality—essentially for the risk that the borrower will default on the loan. The mortgage-writing business runs on narrow profit margins and high volume. For efficiency's sake the quality classification system uses a few easily measured criteria. How much does the applicant make compared to his mortgage payment? How much is the mortgage compared to the assessed value of the home? How big is the down payment? What is the borrower's credit score, etc.?

Because these criteria are so broad and standardized, they leave out a lot of detail. Chesterton wrote that a landlady considering a new boarder would do better examining the content of his philosophy than his bank account. Mortgage companies don't do that. They run the numbers. They are perfectly aware that any given borrower who shows up as a low risk "by the numbers" may turn out to be a very bad risk because of misfortune or even dishonesty. In olden days (forty years ago) local banks and savings and loans might do a somewhat more thorough and personal evaluation of prospective borrowers. But they often made mistakes as well, not only by being too free with the bank's money but by being too close with it, not making loans they probably should have made.

One reason modern mortgage companies can use broad standardized criteria, even knowing they will make some mistakes, is that the modern mortgage company, unlike the Bailey Savings and Loan, will not keep the mortgage. The originator will sell the mortgage into a very large pool of similar mortgages typically held by an investment bank, like Merrill (oops), Bear Sterns (oops, again), or, well, you get the idea. The biggest players by far in this purchasing and repackaging of mortgages are the Federal National Mortgage Association, "Fannie Mae," and the Federal Home Loan Mortgage Corporation, or "Freddie Mac." These quasi-agencies of the federal government were also stupendously profitable corporations until they went broke and were taken over by the government entirely in 2008. Between the two of them, by 2008 Fannie and Freddie either owned outright or insured the interest and principal on nearly half the total U.S. mortgage market of more than $10 trillion at its peak.[2]

For all practical purposes, the mortgage originators, like New Century or Countrywide, were sales offices for Fannie, Freddie, and the big banks. The mortgage originators have little capital of their own and exist only because they know they will be able to sell their mortgages to the big fellows. Often the banks would advance capital to the originators to enable them to hold mortgages during a "warehousing period" while the mortgages were organized into pools. The banks would then buy the pools and "securitize" them. Securitization means nothing more than the rights to the principal and income from the pools are divided into securities, mostly bonds, that can be bought and sold. So claims on different bits of the cash flow from one mortgage or one pool of mortgages can be assigned to different securities with different ultimate owners. Once the pools are securitized, Fannie and Freddie or the investment banks will typically sell the resulting securities to big investors, like your pension fund. (D—n!)

These large pools of mortgages, drawn from borrowers all across the country, were believed to be safer than, say, the loan portfolio of your old-fashioned local bank because they were immune to any purely local shock, such as the biggest employer in town suddenly shutting down.

The result of all this is to make the mortgage industry look more like the insurance industry. Because the mortgage pools are very large, in theory it no longer matters that the ultimate investors know nothing about the thousands of individual borrowers whose mortgages make up the pool. Like insurance companies, the mortgage pool gets the benefit of the law of large numbers. Sure, there will be some bum loans in the group, maybe even bum loans that your local bank officer might have detected and turned down. But, in theory, our accumulated statistical experience shows that across many thousands of mortgages the good will average out with the bad. Overall the default rate of that pool of mortgages will be just about what we expect from loans of whatever broad class they fit into.

In theory, the investor who ultimately buys a share in such a mortgage pool need not exercise any particular insight or judgment or make any hard choices. In effect he simply rents out his money to an enterprise of a well-established risk level and collects the established market rate for taking that risk. Unlike individual mortgages, these big pools of mortgages can be rated by the government-approved ratings agencies like Moody's and

Standard and Poor, which will give them those familiar labels like AAA (almost risk-free), A (a little risk), or BB (don't try this at home). Everybody, or at least every investor in bond markets, knows what those letters mean, or thinks they do. With the rating affixed there is little need to think about the details, especially if the rating is somewhere within the range of "investment grade."

The investor in a mortgage-backed security, in theory, does not need to know anything about Bill's mortgage or Bob's mortgage or whether Bill drinks or Bob is about to lose his job. Mixed into the pool, Bill's and Bob's mortgages simply become part of an "asset class." The creation of a class of investments that will behave in statistically predictable ways excludes the need for judgment of particular cases. Statistical science replaces judgment; the average risk of a class (believed to be well known) replaces the true uncertainty of individual cases.

That's "securitization." Where does structured finance come in? It's the next logical step, really. Imagine a mortgage pool made up mostly of borrowers with problematic credit scores, such as the "subprime" borrowers we heard about so much as the housing market began to implode. Let's say the agencies rate this pool BBB-. And further let's assume that, based on statistical experience, BBB- mortgages have a maximum expected default rate over the life of the mortgage of 10 percent. Since these are 5-year, adjustable-rate mortgages, that is a pretty high default rate. (Imagine if on your block 10 percent of your neighbors lost their homes in five years.) But 10 percent is the maximum—the worst we expect. A more typical outcome might be 3 percent.[3]

An investment bank, say, Merrill Lynch, owns this BBB- pool of mortgages. Merrill wants to sell it off, take the cash, and go do another deal. (Investment banks make a lot of their income through deal flow and the related fees.) But there is not much of a market for BBB- paper at the moment and especially

BBB– mortgage pools. (Traditional buyers of lower-rated paper, including your authors, are a curmudgeonly lot—old men of few illusions typically too suspicious to buy big pools of paper with no transparency to the "underlying" assets below, i.e., the individual mortgages.) But there are lots of buyers for AAA paper, regarded as almost risk-free. China is minting new millionaires every day. Many of those millionaires, and the companies they run, want to keep their cash in dollar-denominated AAA securities: securities with the safest of all ratings denominated in the safest of all currencies. Also, tens of millions of Americans who once put their money in savings banks insured by the federal government now put that cash into money market funds. These funds reinvest that money almost exclusively in AAA paper because investors must have as much faith in their money market funds as they would in a bank. Real banks also buy freight-train loads of AAA securities, especially since international banking standards give preference to such securities over traditional bank investments like directly held mortgages.

Structured finance can do the trick, turning the BBB– pool of mortgages into two (at least) "tranches," one rated AAA and the other rated something below BBB–, maybe BB or even B.

Here's how it's done. Suppose the pool of mortgages is worth a billion dollars and pays an average interest rate of 7 percent, or $70 million a year. These are 5-year mortgages, so the interest sums to $350 million over the life of the pool.[4] Including the principal, the pool thus yields a total cash flow of $1.35 billion over the life of the deal, if no one defaults.

The structured finance impresarios divide the claims on that $1.35 billion in cash flow into an AAA tranche and a B tranche. The AAA tranche sells for $950 million and in return receives an absolute claim on the first $1.15 billion to come in from the entire pool, leaving $200 million for the B tranche. That works out to about a 4 percent annual return for the AAA tranche. That may sound low, but this is now supposedly super-safe AAA paper. Why? Remember the total cash flow expected from the deal if no one defaults is $1.35 billion, $200 million more than is owed to the AAA tranche. Because the AAA tranche has first claim on all cash flow until it collects $1.15 billion, in effect it has a $200 million margin of safety. Even if losses due to default reach $199.99 million, the AAA investors won't lose a dime.

That $200 million of additional cash flow over and above what is owed to the AAA tranche comfortably exceeds the most that the investors believe can be lost on the entire deal, even if defaults hit their maximum historic level of 10 percent. So, statistically speaking, the expected default rate on the $1.15 billion owed to the AAA tranche approaches zero, which is the requirement for AAA paper.

Meanwhile, the B tranche sells for $50 million (remember we needed a total of $1 billion to fund the mortgages) but has a potential 5-year cash flow of $200 million, for an annualized return approaching 60 percent. Sure, the buyer of the B tranche is now absorbing the entire risk of the deal. If defaults hit their maximum historic level, he may even be wiped out. But defaults probably won't hit their maximum level. The buyer of the B tranche is essentially betting that defaults will occur at something less than the worst rate ever, which seems like a reasonable bet for a potential 60 percent annual return.

In real life the deals are much more complicated, but that is the essence. In theory the AAA buyers get super-safe paper. If they are financial institutions that can borrow at bank rates, they can then leverage[5] that paper to get something more than 4 percent. The B buyers get high yield paper in volume without having to paw through a lot of junk themselves, saving both research and transaction costs. And the dealmakers who put it all together get big fees.

As late as the mid-'90s, structured investment vehicles were still rare. In 1990 total U.S. issuance of mortgage-backed securities was approximately $260 billion, but relatively little of that was "structured" in the sense of lesser-rated mortgage pools being turned into higher-rated securities. In 2001 U.S. issuance of mortgage-backed securities exceeded $1.3 trillion. But almost 90 percent of those securities were backed by traditional mortgages given to creditworthy borrowers and so did not need to be "structured" up to AAA. By 2004 the total amount of mortgage-backed securities exceeded $1.8 trillion—but by then roughly 20 percent of the mortgages packed into those securities were "junk" mortgages of some kind, either given to homeowners with bad credit (subprime) or with nontraditional terms, like low down payments and adjustable interest rates (Alt-A). In 2006 new mortgage-backed issues exceeded $2 trillion—and 40 percent of the underlying mortgages were "junk." These were securities no conservative or institutional investor would buy in large quantities unless they were prettied up by the "structuring" process.

Originally the structured finance market was supply-driven. Debt originators, chiefly banks, wishing to clear their balance sheets and generate cash with which they could originate more loans and collect more fees, drove the market by packaging their loans into more liquid vehicles. But as foreign need for AAA paper grew, the market became demand-driven. To meet that demand, the banks and Fannie and Freddie began using more and more junk mortages as the basis for mortgage-backed securities.

Along with the demand for AAA paper, there grew a huge market in structured finance "derivatives." A derivative is any security whose value depends directly on the value of another security. A stock option is a derivative because its value is "derived" from the price of the stock the option holder has a right to buy or sell. The dominant derivative in the asset-backed securities market is the credit default swap, or CDS. A credit default swap is a pure bet on the creditworthiness of some other debt security. Let's say Jim owes Jack $1 billion on a bond Jim issued and Jack bought. That's their business. Meanwhile Bill and Bob make a bet over whether Jim will pay on time. If he does, Bill wins and Bob pays; if he doesn't, Bob wins and Bill pays. Neither Bill nor Bob knows either Jim or Jack, and they have no direct involvement with the original bond. That's a credit default swap.

Tradable indices of asset-backed securities became another derivative. As with, for instance, a tradable index of the S&P 500, these allowed investors to bet on the market as a whole rather than on individual asset-backed securities.

While the structured finance market grew so did its influence over the price of traditional credit instruments such as commercial bonds, and thus over interest rates. In a lengthy (and very enthusiastic) report on the influence of structured finance on credit markets, the International Monetary Fund concluded that "credit derivative markets increasingly influence loan pricing. . . .The growing importance of credit derivatives in setting the marginal price of credit, including bank loans, suggests that credit derivatives may influence credit markets even more than bonds." [6]

The IMF wasn't criticizing. Like most major institutional players, including most of the regulatory agencies and the central banks and governments of the major economic powers, the IMF celebrated the emergence of the new instruments. It regarded mortgage-backed securities and derivatives as preferable to old-fashioned bank loans precisely because they could be traded in public or quasi-public securities markets. The IMF applauded "this continued evolution from primarily a bank-based financial system to a more market-based system" wherein "deeper, more efficient, and liquid credit markets" would "make more transparent the volatility inherent in credit, which was previously masked by bank balance sheets." [7]

Wait a minute, we hear you ask, what did the IMF mean by saying that it was good to move away from a bank-based system and toward a "market-based system"? Don't banks operate in a market?

When an institution like the IMF says "markets" in a context like this it means public securities markets, open to all bidders (or at least many bidders). According to the contemporary ideology of finance, larger, more public markets are always more "efficient" (more likely to get prices right) than smaller, more private markets or individual buyers and sellers, like the loan officer at your local bank. Broad public markets are supposed to save the economy from the erratic judgment of local loan officers or even objective local factors—like a local recession—that might constrain local banks. Also in a public market anyone can "vote" (by buying or selling) on what a collection of mortgages is worth. Under the old system where banks held their loans instead of turning them into public securities, only the auditors (from the banks or the regulators) had the power to say that a loan on the bank's books should be marked down in value because it had become more risky. The bank would have to report such markdowns, but the decision was made behind closed doors. The IMF was arguing that by turning bank loans into securities tradable on public markets the process of deciding what those loans were worth would become transparent—a public event.

The mortgage-backed securities market never became nearly as "public" as the stock market, where many stocks trade hundreds or thousands of times in a day. Even at its height the mortgage-backed securities market was more like the more rarified regions of the corporate bond market wherein many bonds trade less than once a day. Still it had the essential elements of any public securities market: Market participants bought and sold more or less standardized securities representing claims on assets about which neither buyer nor seller had much information. And, as in securities markets generally, prices were mostly set not by analysis and negotiation about the value of a particular asset but by what other traders had most recently paid for the same or similar securities.

The securities created by structured finance were sold as being easier to understand and having far more predictable future performance than the underlying mortgages that went into them. Think again about insurance. The idea of fire insurance is that the insurance company and its investors can have a much better idea of what percentage of a million houses will burn down than it (or anyone) can have of whether your particular house will burn down.

In buying insurance, you spread or "diversify" the risk of your house burning down across all the houses in the insurance company's portfolio, turning great particular uncertainty into a broadly predictable percentage. As with all insurance schemes, you are substituting diversification for knowledge. If you had perfect knowledge that your house would not burn down, you would not need to diversify away your risk by buying insurance.

This great virtue of any diversification scheme is also its vice. By compensating for ignorance, diversification can make knowledge and expertise seem unnecessary. The great effect of structured finance, its very purpose, was to persuade large, conservative institutional investors who would never have purchased lower-grade securities that they could now do so because those securities had been transformed into AAAs. Even better, they could invest without inquiring into the details of the underlying mortgages "down below."

Normally, troubled or troubling securities such as high yield or "junk" bonds are bought by experts—trouble is their business. They diversify also, but they mostly depend on a close analysis of what they are buying. But the investors who bought the bulk of this new structured paper were conservative institutions (including the banks and Fannie and Freddie, which not only did the securitization but bought much of the resulting paper for their own portfolios). Most of these conservative institutions would never have been willing or even legally allowed to own directly the pools of lower-grade assets from which the "structured" AAA tranches were created. They lacked the skill or inclination to analyze the underlying assets and bought into the structured products only because they were persuaded they did not need to do any such analysis.

In December of 2005 the *Journal of Structured Finance* conducted a survey of its readers asking how they defined structured finance. The list of suggested definitions included several like this one: "A way to pool assets together . . . to be sold to investors who otherwise would not want to purchase the underlying assets."[8]

As we wrote at the time, in the event of a disturbance in credit markets, these staid institutional buyers' sudden realization that they had no idea what they owned "could easily turn to panic. Many of them have relied largely on the ratings agencies for reassurance. But the ratings agencies that cover structured finance are necessarily relying on unseasoned valuation models likely to go haywire under stress."

Translation: conservative investors who vastly overestimated the quality of the structured paper they had bought could, in the face of a crisis, quickly stampede into vastly underestimating it.

Convincing institutional investors to buy these novel securities was quite difficult at first. Early investors typically required the investment banks putting together the deals to "eat their own cooking" by retaining the highest-risk tranches in their own portfolios. But as structured vehicles became accepted and the demand for AAA paper (as well as the supposedly transparent, diversified, and predictable lower-grade paper formed from the lower tranches) grew, soon even conservative investors were beating a path to the bankers' doors.

One of the principal virtues of the structured finance market (in the view of its advocates) was precisely that structuring made it possible for a flock of new, inexperienced investors to buy debt once held only by experts. As one cheerleading-industry publication wrote, structured finance "has given the world access to a market that was previously the purview of a handful of players with the expertise to evaluate B-notes, bridge loans, or mezzanine debt," enabling "buyers with limited real estate expertise to rely on rating agency assessments of the top tranches in" structured finance vehicles.[9]

The International Monetary Fund (IMF) put matters even more bluntly. In the structured and derivative credit markets, it proclaimed, the biggest, most experienced banks sell risk, while smaller banks and other conservative institutions buy it. "In the past, banks generally warehoused credit risk, seeking to provision against losses as the economy and the credit cycle evolved. . . . Today . . . banks increasingly prefer to act as credit originators and to transfer credit exposures to others via the capital markets."[10]

So banks were making loans that they knew they would sell off, sticking others with any defaults. Did the IMF here catch a whiff of moral hazard (as insurance companies call incentives to commit fraud)? Heaven forbid! The IMF went so far as to acknowledge the possibility but then dismissed it with the astonishing claim that market discipline would operate faultlessly even at the level of individual firms: "[T]he banks most active in these risk transfer markets must, for continued market access, preserve their market credibility, and therefore they are unlikely to seek a short-term gain with much greater long-term costs."[11]

If this logic held, we would never have had Enron or World-Com. Your humble authors are unabashed free-market capitalists and proud of it. We are staunch Republicans who believe Ronald Reagan was the greatest president in our lifetimes. We firmly believe that the market, like the Lord, punishes the wicked eventually. But like the Lord, the market acts in its own good time, respecting the free will and the potential for misery-making of even the most depraved souls. Market discipline provides little immediate protection against any single fraud—or even an epidemic of frauds driven by a novel moral hazard.

Crucial to persuading once-conservative investors to invest in junk mortgages tricked out as AAA paper were the government-approved ratings agencies such as Moody's and Standard and Poor. These agencies use standardized models to score the creditworthiness of various securities. This works well enough when the models are reasonably simple and applied to security types that have been around for generations. But the models for assessing structured finance paper were complex and based on necessarily untested assumptions.

No one had adequate data on the prior performance of either structured finance products as a class or many of the novel types of underlying mortgages, which had never before existed in any volume. To generate statistics on the historic behavior of an asset class, you need, well, some history. Nobody had any. As we wrote in the summer of 2006, "There is no precedent in the mortgage market for the indifference to credit risk enabled by the current generation of [mortgage-backed securities]. Try searching for historic precedents for the performance of 'no-documentation,' 'stated income,' FICO-score-620 [adjustable-rate] mortgages . . . in an environment of flat-to-down housing prices. The available data set is zero on several counts."

Even worse, a huge proportion of subprime mortgages were not for home purchases but for "cash-out refinancings." In a "cash-out refi" the homeowner refinances his house not against the original purchase price but against the most recent assessment of its supposed market value in a rising housing market. And then often as not, the borrower uses the money to buy a boat or an RV. Refinancings entail considerably greater moral hazard—incentives to commit fraud—than new home purchases. A homebuyer has some incentive to keep the appraisal on his new house low because appraisals roughly limit prices. In a cash-out refinancing, the borrower and mortgage broker alike want the appraisal to be as high as they can convince the appraiser to make it. And since there is no actual sale in a refi, the appraisals are based exclusively on estimates that naturally become hugely flexible on the upside. In the land of the cash-out refi, every home is above average. As we wrote at the time, "think of mortgage credits of this quality—homeowners who cannot support their lifestyles on their incomes but must dig into capital to stay current—as failing businesses. Businesses that over the long term cannot service their debts out of operating income are appropriately rated triple-C credits and quite commonly have default rates of 50 percent over the course of a few years, with correspondingly high loss ratios."

Even the IMF in its otherwise wildly enthusiastic report noted at the time that "detailed data on structured credit products are not readily available and relatively few studies have been done so far on the broader financial stability implications of these credit risk transfer markets." In addition ". . . there remains a paucity of data for public authorities to more quantitatively assess the degree of risk reduction among banks and to monitor where the credit risk has gone."[12]

Not to worry. The only real danger the IMF saw from this gap in understanding was that it might "cause some analysts, researchers, and policymakers to *underestimate* the benefits of these markets."[13] (Emphasis added.)

In 2005 Professor Frank J. Fabozzi of Yale University released a study finding the models for rating structured finance paper were dangerously unreliable. The models could not, for example, reliably predict what percentage of structured securities, especially mortgage-backed securities, would go into default. "Default modeling for ABS [asset-backed securities] is in its infancy," he wrote—in part because investors in these securities believed the structuring process had rendered the prospects of default almost irrelevant. "For most asset classes, credit enhancement is viewed as sufficient to insulate senior class holders from credit exposure." In other words, the AAA buyers, who typically accounted for 90 percent of the investment, were relying on the assumption that any defaults would be absorbed by the lower tranches. They did not push the rating agencies to come up with better models because they thought the very structure of the deal made traditional credit analysis irrelevant.[14]

Another reason default models for mortgage-backed securities developed slowly, Fabozzi pointed out, was that many were built from mortgage types with no meaningful default history of their own. Interest-only adjustable-rate mortgages were an exotic product until the late 1990s. Yet as Fabozzi stated, adjustable-rate mortgages, including interest-only adjustable-rate mortgages, were an extremely popular raw material for mortgage-backed securities. "Yet as of this writing, no data are available to allow a thorough analysis of the credit risk for th[is] largest sector of the residential ABS [asset-backed securities] market."[15]

Even more dangerously unreliable, as it turned out, would be the models used to predict the *market valuation* of mortgage-backed securities. Market valuation means simply the price for which a security can be readily sold at any given moment in a public or quasi-public market. The stock quotes you see running beneath the CNBC screen are "market valuations." A generation ago such momentary market valuations were irrelevant to the mortgage market and most of the banking business. A bank's balance sheet, and thus its own creditworthiness, could be undermined by deteriorating mortgages. But that deterioration would be measured by a far more deliberate process than a public market's minute-by-minute guess at value.

Once mortgages began to be "securitized" and either traded directly in public markets, or used as the basis for derivative securities that were so traded, it was inevitable that investors and regulators would evaluate banks that held large portfolios of such securities based on the market value of those securities. A bank whose liabilities exceed its assets is insolvent. If its insolvency cannot be readily healed, investors will abandon it, creditors will pursue it, and regulators will shut it down. Under the new regime, even banks that seemed to be in the highly traditional, conservative business of lending money on real estate could be solvent one minute and insolvent another based on the shifting moods of public markets and the shifting market prices of mortgage-backed securities.

For this reason, models to predict the market valuation of mortgage-backed securities became crucial. Fabozzi was even more pessimistic about the emerging valuation models than he was about the default models. Even if these new valuation models turned out to be sound under ordinary circumstances, he worried that in times of market stress, they were likely to drastically mislead. One danger was that even models that did a good job of predicting average prices over time would not do a good job predicting extreme prices (for instance during a panic) that might be subsumed in the average. The typical valuation model "does not incorporate changes in market liquidity," Fabozzi pointed out. (Liquidity, or cash, tends to disappear in a panic.) Already, in the spring of 1994, similar models had failed for this very reason, he explained.[16]

Consider two bonds. As with most bonds, "par," or full payoff value, is 100. One bond always sells at between 90 and 100, averages 95, and ends its life paying off at par. The other bond also averages 95 and also ends its life at par. But for a few panicky weeks (say in the fall of 2008) the price drops to 60, a price that suggests a very high risk of default. Fabozzi was saying essentially that the models could not predict which of those two "pathways" a structured bond would take in a general panic. "But it is precisely the proclivity of the structured finance market to produce a panic that concerns us" (as we wrote at the time). In such a panic, even banks holding mortgage securities that might ultimately survive and pay off in full might appear broke because their balance sheets would briefly be full of bonds that had lost much of their market value.

Of course the opposite problem existed as well: It is almost certain that banks that were being given clean bills of health by markets and regulators alike throughout 2006 and the first half of 2007 were in grave danger and ought to have been seized by the government and closed. But those banks were able to report strong balance sheets as late as summer of 2007 because public markets were still valuing at par mortgage securities that would lose more than half their market value within months.

The proponents of the efficient market hypothesis love modern financial markets precisely because they move at light speed, evaluating new information from moment to moment and turning on a dime. Sounds great, but when all that racing around is being done in the dark you can end up with a heck of a crash.

CHAPTER THREE

New Risks in Old Bottles

The risks faced by an investor in public financial markets are either "systemic" or "idiosyncratic." Systemic risk is the risk that all the securities in an entire market will move up and down together because of some powerful outside force, including the psychology of the market. If three-quarters of the stocks on the New York Stock Exchange go down on the same day, you are watching systemic risk in action. Idiosyncratic risk is just the reverse. The world is beautiful, the economy is humming along, stocks are going up everywhere, but the CFO of Fly By Night Industries announces that its newest product, doesn't, um, fly. FBN's stock drops like a stone while everyone else's is rising. That's idiosyncratic risk.[17]

The great mission of modern investment theory is to replace all idiosyncratic risk with systemic risk. Modern theory says, essentially, it is impossible for investors to be consistently better than the market at predicting the fortunes of individual securities like the stock of Fly By Night. So it's pointless and even dangerous to try. But based on historical statistics, says the modern theory, we can reliably estimate the probable long-term performance of an entire class of investments. Using this information we can build portfolios that are appropriately diversified to accurately represent various asset classes, with well-known risks and returns. By building portfolios that accurately represent known asset classes, we can be sure of what risks we are taking and how much we are going to be paid for taking them. The primary skill of finance, under this theory, becomes diversification, which becomes an advanced statistical methodology for making sure a relatively small number of securities accurately represents a much larger class of securities. The ultimate diversified portfolio would reflect the risk and return of the entire world economy: the "world portfolio." There is no larger class to diversify into: you can't buy insurance against the end of the world.

Now, diversification is important to any good investor—it's what we substitute for knowledge. Since our knowledge always falls short to some degree, some degree of diversification is always essential. I may know, or believe I know, a lot about the prospects of Company A, enough to prompt me to invest in it heavily. But I can't know *everything* (which includes the future), so I don't bet *everything*. I also invest in companies B, C, and D, on which I also think I have a good handle. The less I know, the more I need to diversify. If I had perfect knowledge, I would own only one security at any given moment—the one that would make the most money for me in that moment. If I know nothing, my need for diversification is infinite.

Modern investment theory in effect says we know nothing. It is impossible (or very improbable) for an investor to value any given security more accurately than the market does. So all investment strategy is subsumed in diversification. All investment consists of resolving the uncertainty of individual cases not by making judgments about those individual cases but by fitting those cases into a class, wherein the law of large numbers prevails. All investment is reduced to insurance.

This is not a wholly stupid idea, but it conceals several grave dangers.

The first, which has received lots of attention lately, is the so-called "fat tails" problem—the tendency for extreme events to happen more often than random chance would suggest. The extreme left and right "tails" of a bell curve, representing the probability of extreme events, turn out to be thicker—"fatter"—than expected. Translation: the world portfolio is not as stable as it seems. Catastrophic market events, hundred-year floods, happen more often than they should. Exposing oneself to the risk of the entire system may turn out to be just as dangerous as trying to beat the market by "picking winners." Moreover, the more investors invest by asset class rather than by picking individual companies, the more the market will tend to move as one, intensifying herd behavior and the likelihood of panics, making hundred-year floods even more likely.

The second danger is that diversification, too aggressively used as a substitute for knowledge, ultimately undermines diversification itself. A poorly understood portfolio may be far less diversified than it appears to be. This is exactly what happened in the mortgage debacle. Big banks like Citi and Merrill disastrously concentrated in novel mortgage-backed securities and derivatives, precisely because they believed the diversification within the pools made them safe. They felt safe because they knew they were not overcommitted to Bill's mortgage as opposed to Bob's mortgage, or even to mortgages from Peoria as opposed to Pittsburgh. They were invested in mortgages generally. Even better, they were invested in a diverse selection of mortgages that shared one thing on common—by virtue of the structuring of the pool into tranches, all their mortgages were effectively AAA.

The problem was that their apparently diversified mortgage portfolios were actually dangerously correlated. Correlated means that the performance of many apparently diverse investments in a portfolio will actually track—be correlated to—a single risk factor like the weather or the unemployment rate. Too many of your investments, however diverse they might look, actually share some crucial variable.

Now of course the banks knew that by concentrating in mortgages they were accepting heavy exposure to the variables *traditionally* associated with mortgages, the systemic risk of the mortgage market rather than the idiosyncratic risk that Bill or Bob would default. A rise in unemployment across the nation, for instance, will generally increase mortgage defaults and foreclosures. But these historically tracked risks were both well known and small. Although individual mortgages don't get rated, traditional mortgages behave pretty much like AAA bonds even in an economic downturn. On average, default rates are miniscule. And banks had always concentrated in mortgages. Given that banks concentrate their investments in mortgages anyway, they believed they had improved matters by fully insuring against the small traditional risks of the mortgage market by offloading those risks onto the lower-rated tranches.

Unfortunately, the structured securities market had created new risk variables that the old models did not take into account. As a result, many mortgage pools turned out to be less diversified than your old local bank's loan portfolio. When we started to bet massively against the mortgage market in early 2006, one of our colleagues at Whitebox dug into the underlying components of various mortgage-backed securities looking for bad ones we could bet against. Again and again he discovered dangerous correlations of a sort never before tracked by the industry. One statistic we found extremely useful was the percentage of mortgages in a given pool that were written by the most obviously crooked mortgage originators—the ones most likely to have accepted or even solicited phony documentation, to have puffed-up assessments, and otherwise gamed the system. It was possible to sort mortgage-backed securities by whether most of the mortgages in them were written by crooks or by relatively honest dealers. (Even in 2005 and probably earlier, it was obvious who the crooks were. There are a lot of people out there who need to go to jail.)

Another variable that had never been central to the mortgage business before but now became crucial was housing prices. Foreclosure rates on 30-year, 20 percent down, fixed-rate mortgages are not very sensitive to housing prices. The homeowner has borrowed the money for the life of a mortgage and at the maturity of that mortgage he will own the house outright. He does not have to go back to the bank again in three years and get his loan renewed. So even if housing prices drop, it's practically irrelevant whether the market price of the house is now "under water" compared to the mortgage—unless the owner for his own reasons must sell. And if he does have to sell, 20 percent down is usually plenty of cushion for the bank precisely because in a world of 20 percent down, 30-year mortgages, housing prices tend to be fairly steady.

Much different is a low down payment, 3-year, variable-rate mortgage resulting from a refinancing made in a booming housing market. That "cash-out" refinancing may effectively reduce the owner's equity in the house to 5 or 10 percent of the current market value (or less if the assessment was pumped up to get the deal done). When such loans become common, housing prices become the biggest factor in default and foreclosure rates. Now millions of homeowners must refinance within three or five years, and none will be able to if housing prices drop. Housing prices control the fate of every mortgaged-backed security built from pools of such "innovative" mortgages.

In the end, though, the single most dangerous correlation was not an objective factor shared by various mortgage-backed securities but a subjective one shared by the vast majority of investors in them: ignorance of what they owned. Ignorance is the father of panic. Ignorance makes for credulous and overconfident buyers on the way up. But it really takes over on the way down when investors suddenly realize they have not a clue what they own. They start selling not because they learn that the security they own is chock-full of bum loans from crooked dealers but because they don't know that it isn't. We don't mean to be too blasé about how bad some of the mortgage paper out there was. When the market, in 2007, started pricing the lower-rated tranches of mortgage-backed securities down close to zero, the market seems to have been dead right, just a year or two late. It was clear even earlier that defaults would be bad enough to wipe out much of that paper. But remember, the low-rated tranches, technically, can go to zero without the AAA tranches losing a dime. When the crisis came, the problem that led to panic was that the market had no way to readily determine whether any given "AAA" tranche was going to lose a dime or a dollar or half its value. They simply became unacceptable to own, impossible to sell, except to that relatively small part of the bond market that is comfortable analyzing troubled securities.

In this sense, the mortgage crisis was a special case of a general problem with diversification, the "common ownership problem." Suppose financial markets are dominated by, oh, fifty big institutional investors, all of which manage their portfolios according to the modern theory. They all diversify into well-known asset classes. Which means . . . these highly diversified bedrock companies all own the same things! If a few of those fifty institutional investors hit a crisis and need to sell off to raise cash, all the others will also see a sudden drop in value as everyone's portfolio moves down together, possibly creating a domino effect and a market spasm, or worse.

As structured finance came to dominate debt markets, even many firms that had traditionally maintained strong departments of credit analysts began to de-emphasize them. The more that insurance schemes came to dominate the game, the thinner the analyst ranks became. As a result, when the panic eventually did come, there were few firms with sufficient confidence in their own judgment to buy even the better mortgage-backed securities. No one wanted to know from better or worse. As we wrote at the time, in the event "the big conservative investors who have plunged into structured instruments begin to panic who would be on the other side of the trade? After a decade of propaganda about structure and diversification mooting analysis, there is now a stark mismatch between the number and variety of credits that would fall as one in the event of a crisis and the relatively small and shrinking corps of good credit men with sleeves up-rolled and calculators charged, ready to catch the good ones as they fall. We'll be there, but we expect to be lonely. . . . The current fashion in structured finance is going to come to an end—like all fashions—and when it does it will end badly. It will end badly not only because investors have been absurdly optimistic about default and recovery rates under stress but because the very power and pervasiveness of structured finance have stripped away the infrastructure needed to cope with a panic."

The great goal of "securitization" of the mortgage market had been achieved. Just as the cheerleaders at the IMF and essentially every major regulatory institution, major government, money-center bank, and academic department of finance had hoped and advocated, mortgages were being bought and sold in the same brilliantly efficient, high-tech, computerized, whizz-bang, go-go sort of public markets as publicly held stocks and bonds. After decades, nay centuries, of stodgy, retrograde, primitive, stick-in-the-mud behavior, finally mortgage markets could panic too.

CHAPTER FOUR

The Misinformation Economy

How should we think about panic? The events of our lifetimes as well as the financial history of the U.S. show that financial panics are almost routine. For the baby boom generation of investors, "hundred-year floods" have come at least once a decade. Less than five years separated October 2002 (roughly the bottom of the tech wreck) from the visible onset of the mortgage crisis.

One way to think about panic is as a general, nonspecific response to a poorly understood particular and specific problem. As in the fight or flight reflex, sometimes this response is helpful, and sometimes it isn't. Apparently if you happen upon a grizzly bear in the wild you are absolutely not supposed to run. There is something specific you are supposed to do: we both remember reading about it. But we can't remember what it is: it was too specific. Meanwhile, the proper response to crossing paths with a rattlesnake apparently is quite different. (Running seems more plausible, which suggests that panicking is not always wrong.)

When people reflect on their actions in a panic they often

say things like, "I didn't think, I just panicked." Or sometimes they say, "I didn't know what to do, so I ran." Panic is provoked by information failure. Maybe we actually had the information to deal with the problem, but in the grip of fear we could not process it ("I didn't think, I just panicked"). Or maybe we simply did not have the information ("I didn't know what to do, so I ran").

If some amazing disaster strikes the economy, like nuclear war, and the Dow drops to 50, that may be a sensible response to very unhappy information. But a real panic is usually driven by missing or unprocessed information.

On the other hand, clear thinking depends on limiting information, sorting the wheat from the chaff. Most human thought is conceptual—it requires abstraction. A basketball, a baseball, and a golf ball yield the concept "ball"; a stop sign, a rose, and a fire truck yield the concept "red." Now we can think of a red ball, or even make one. Only by dropping most of the information in these individual objects can we find these useful concepts.

Models, including financial models, work only because they shed certain information in order to highlight or analyze other information. This is necessarily true. A great physicist once summed up the situation: "To build a perfect model of the universe would require all the matter and energy in the universe, because the only perfect model, the only model that shed no information and made no compromises in order to achieve its object, would be the universe itself."[18]

This is the virtue of models: They exclude information not directly relevant to the question under consideration, allowing us to focus on the significance of particular variables.

This is also the vice of models: If the discarded information proves decisive to the issue being analyzed, the model will fail. If the model fails in a critical situation, and the people using the model cannot recover or even identify the critical lost information, they may not be able to react rationally to events; they may panic.

The mortgage meltdown can be understood as an instance of model failure. Investors had been persuaded that the models driving structured finance were a sufficient basis for trusting that AAA paper really was safe. When some of that supposedly invulnerable paper began to deteriorate, proving the models worthless, investors fled en masse.

There have always been financial crises. Contemporary investment theory did not create them. But the very high level of abstraction at which statistical finance operates—the large amounts of information stripped away, for instance, in order to turn individual mortgages on Bill's house or Bob's house into microcomponents of several different securities—does tend to create crises of lost information. Most of the market seizures we have seen over the last forty years or so have fallen in this category. Probably the clearest example, and the one that most closely parallels the mortgage crunch, was the great crash of October 1987.

As we mentioned in chapter two, Andrew predicted the crash of 1987 just as he predicted the credit market collapse of 2007–2008. The only difference was that, whereas we actually published his prediction of the credit collapse, Andrew's article predicting the '87 crash, submitted to a magazine in July of that year, lay moldering in an editor's drawer until November of 1987 when it was decided to publish it as a retrospective. If you guessed that Richard was the unfortunate editor in question, go to the head of the class.

The root cause of the '87 crash, as Andy wrote at the time and as we still believe today, was the advent of "equities futures" markets. An equities futures contract is essentially a pure bet on the future price of a basket of stocks—an asset class—such as the collection of 500 major companies included in the S&P 500 index.[19]

Equities futures markets, like derivative markets more generally, were made possible by computers. But they drew their inspiration from agriculture. An S&P futures contract is a security that aspires to the condition of a pork belly. In that aspiration the humble S&P contract is fated to eternal frustration.

Consider the pig. Or for simplicity consider that even more humble precursor of the pig, the bushel of corn. (We are assuming well-fed pigs.) Now a bushel of corn is a fine thing in many ways. True, it lacks niacin. But otherwise it is a perfectly decent nutrient as grains go and admirably tasty compared to some of its blander cousins. But however rich in taste, corn—like other grains—is undeniably poor in information. Even if it were true (and we have no information to the contrary) that each kernel of corn, like every snowflake, is an utterly unique creation, still, all in all, one is very like another. When one buys a bushel of corn of a certain USDA grade, or a million bushels for future delivery on an exchange, one knows, with a precision satisfactory for all normal purposes, exactly what one is getting.

As Claude Shannon, father of information theory, taught us, information is differentiation; information is what comes as a surprise against the background of knowledge already possessed. The next kernel, indeed the next bushel or million bushels of corn, provides remarkably little information against the background of the kernels that preceded it. In short, corn is a commodity. Commodity markets are markets in assets with minimal information content, which information therefore can be formalized without great loss. A corn futures contract is an abstraction. But it is an abstraction from which little has been abstracted, for the simple reason that a bushel of corn contains little information to begin with.

The invention of the S&P future was an attempt to turn shares of complex, information-rich companies into a single, simple commodity by combining the law of large numbers with the magic of diversification. This effort was part and parcel of the mission of modern investment theory, which is to persuade investors to disavow any attempt to make value judgments about the underlying assets or companies. Instead, we are to treat investment in complex companies as we do investment in simple grains of corn—as an essentially statistical exercise. Just as corn traders can practice their trade in blissful ignorance of the condition of any particular kernel, so stock shares that once seemed to represent claims on the particular assets and liabilities of a very particular business were to be treated simply as bits in a bushel.

There is, alas, a yawning difference between corn futures and equity index futures. Both convey only modest amounts of information to the buyer. In the case of the corn, there was never much information to lose. But in the case of an equity index, the fall-off in information content between the individual complex company (about which significant if not sufficient information is available to even the public investor) and the abstraction is enormous.

If uncertainty and risk are nearly synonyms, then information (or knowledge, which is simply information previously captured) and risk are nearly opposites. Information-poor markets are by definition highly speculative markets—as commodity markets, despite their very real economic purpose, have always been. Corn prices are notoriously set by unknowable future macro events, weather being the most notorious. Almost all the information about the future price of a kernel of corn is to be found in the future not in the corn. Untethered to existing information, corn futures prices are necessarily speculative.[20] The weather, the economy, and all sorts of external factors also affect Wal-Mart and K-Mart, Toyota and GM. But unlike kernels of corn, these companies are active agents responding to these external factors. Their ability to respond is represented, however inadequately, by the information available, for instance, in their public financial statements.

Even before index futures, equity markets were prone to panic. Rumor, greed, and fear could overwhelm existing knowledge. Defenders of equity futures argued that, as in commodity markets, the real economic purpose of a futures contract was to provide insurance from unpredictable market shocks. Index futures would allow investors to invest in their insight about individual companies and hedge their bet by shorting the market as a whole. They could make the well-informed specific judgment about an individual company while hedging against general market moves that might overwhelm company-level developments. Like insurance, equity futures were merely tools to make the real business safer.

Instead, under the influence of modern investment theory (inadvertently magnified by the primitive automated computer trading of the day), the tool consumed the market and speculation overwhelmed investment. As Andrew wrote in that 1987 article,

> The futures market now leads the stock market, and stock-index futures have turned individual stocks into short-term speculative bets as well. The very existence of [index futures] encourages the stocks themselves to be traded in baskets and to react very sensitively to any news that might have an impact on the market as a whole. Every trader in America knows, or thinks he knows, that a decline in the futures market means someone is about to unload a big bundle of stocks, and traders act accordingly, dumping whole groups of potentially affected stocks before they get dumped on. Under even the best conditions stock prices tend to herd; trading in index futures increases the herding instinct. Betting on individual stocks [has become] unacceptably risky in an environment in which underlying values are constantly being overwhelmed by broad market moves.

On a short-term basis, stocks have become much less independent of each other than in the past, making a sharp decline and subsequent panic more likely. It is not particularly unusual for all thirty stocks in the Dow to go up or down at the same time; that rarely happened when market participants were interested in the value of individual companies. The zero-sum character of the game rewards and virtually guarantees manipulation, deception, and illegality. Add a high degree of leverage to the equation, and the scene is set for disaster.

In such an environment, all the subsequent debate about the proximate cause of the 1987 panic was pointless. As George Soros has pointed out, the proximate cause of a panic is never the real cause any more than the last straw actually breaks the camel's back. As the notion of equities as kernels in a commodity bushel gained power, the preponderance of equity traders felt relieved from the obligation of looking their stocks too closely in the belly. As a result, when panic struck, very little of the institutional money was sitting with the traditional bargain hunters, the guys for whom a stock was still a claim on a particular business. There was no one to stop the slide by discerning value in individual stocks.

One reason the mortgage crunch was so predictable was that by 2006 credit markets were in the same condition. The slower pace of trading on bond markets (nothing like the hair-trigger program trading that sped the 1987 crash along!) merely disguised the extent to which speculation had replaced investment as deal structure replaced information and analysis. In both 1987 and 2006, investors believed that diversification made their holdings safer. In both cases, the diversification they relied on was largely illusory. No matter how diverse the companies in an index are, if the indices themselves dominate the market, then all the securities in the index do indeed share one fateful "shadow" correlation. They are all members of the index, and it is the index, not the companies, that the market is trading.

Similarly, the greatest danger in a credit market dominated by structured finance was not the hidden correlations within any given mortgage-backed security (such as a high proportion of mortgages originated by crooks), though these were dangerous enough. The greatest danger was that a dominant set of complex and opaque securities had taken the market hostage, securities about which their owners knew just enough to be terrified once that market began to crack. In both cases, the most profound correlations were to ignorance and fear.

Just as the core theory of equity indexing was that diversification could substitute for exhaustive (and perhaps unreliable) analysis of the underlying companies, the core theory of structured finance was that by combining large piles of individual credits into tradable securities, the packager would eliminate the need for a great deal of expensive and imprecise valuation of individual credits. Once again, thanks to the magic of diversification, a few highly formalized (i.e., information-impoverished) metrics substituted for actually knowing which mortgages one was buying.

The essence of modern investment theory is to ascend to a level of abstraction that makes fallible individual judgments irrelevant. Unfortunately, in the course of rendering such judgments irrelevant, one may also make them impossible. Climbing the ladder of abstraction, one inevitably sheds a heavy burden of information. At 30,000 feet, every security on the ground looks like every other. In 2007, as in 1987, just when it became most urgent to sort the good from the bad, it would become practically impossible for most investors to do so. The only option left was to run like hell, which is one sure-fire way to get et by a bear.

PART II
The Ideology Of Modern Finance

CHAPTER FIVE

The Reign of Risk

The ideology that for more than a generation has dominated theory and practice of investing in public securities markets has a name. It is called "modern portfolio theory" or "the MPT" for short. Originally based on the best available data and the most sophisticated academic research, in recent decades the empirical case for modern portfolio theory has steadily eroded. On the practical side, not only have hedge fund managers, who generally reject the theory, gotten superior results, but repeated financial-market catastrophes during the MPT's reign have shaken it to its foundation. And yet the modern theory, or at least its central philosophical intuition, continues to dominate securities markets and especially institutional portfolios. Why does such an evidently discredited, damaging, and dangerous idea continue to wield such power?

Modern portfolio theory was a late bloom of the great eighteenth and nineteenth century impulse to explain human society by mechanical or "scientific" principles as regular as those of classical physics. This aspiration has been especially strong in economics. Smith's metaphor of the invisible hand expressed the idea that the established mechanisms of markets—of which no single market player need be conscious—direct an enormous portion of economic activity. The farmer tends to plant roughly as much wheat as the baker can buy at a price profitable to them both without either knowing anything about the other.

Markets are mechanisms that express the economic implications of vast amounts of information and accumulated wisdom without anyone having to do any centralized information processing, either in a mind or in a computer model. Like the solar system, or evolution, markets work without "knowing." Like a remarkable number of the most useful human institutions, they are substitutes for thought. The resulting efficiencies, in the classical view, largely explain why free economies trounce planned economies.

Alas, fixating on the very real economic benefits of not thinking tends to obscure the importance of that other great source of wealth: thinking. Economists have always been much better at explaining the unconscious mechanisms of markets than the conscious work of entrepreneurship and innovation. Entrepreneurship is not only the other side of capitalism, it is the opposite side. Entrepreneurship can be understood as a force that disrupts markets by introducing new information or a more accurate judgment about economic value.

The great achievement of markets is to reduce the need to make judgments in the face of uncertainty. This is why market economies are contrasted to planned economies. Economic planners claim to know too much. They make too many judgments. Their reach exceeds their grasp. Central planning, like most rationalist schemes, is a form of hubris.

Yet even in free markets challenges arise that require judgment. Entrepreneurship consists in making correctly those judgments that remain necessary even in free markets, thereby introducing innovations that change the economic landscape. The reward for making these judgments well is called profit.

Classical economic theory has generally held the view that the better (i.e., the more completely informed) a market, the less need for the entrepreneur. In a perfect market, entrepreneurship and true profit would disappear. Workers, managers, and investors would all still make a living: they would be compensated at market rates for their routine inputs. All costs, including the cost of capital, would be covered. But there would be no "extra" payment for new ideas showing how to make more out of less. There would be no need for new ideas because everybody would already know everything. In an economy of perfect knowledge the market serves as a perfect computer of cost and compensation. Inputs are compensated, but insights are not—because there is no need of them.

Modern portfolio theory is an extreme example of the tendency of economists to focus on the mechanics of markets, which can be readily quantified, and pay very little attention to entrepreneurship, which is almost impossible to speak about in formal terms. If economics were about entrepreneurship, it would not look like physics. It would look a little like philosophy. Mostly it would look like literature.

Essentially, modern portfolio theory says that public financial markets, being nearly perfect, determine what to pay their investors for their necessarily routine inputs. Markets determine this payment so powerfully that investors can do little or nothing to improve their results above the average. For most investors, attempting to behave entrepreneurially is as productive as trying to climb out of quicksand—you are better off just staying still.

In one sentence, the core of the modern theory is that investors are paid the market return for the risks they take. Risk, in this view, is a standard "input" perfectly priced by the market. The more risk, the more return. That is not to say that the way to get rich is to take insane risks. There is a science to risk taking;

modern portfolio theory is that science. Applying the principles of MPT, investors can engineer a portfolio such that they have a reasonable expectation of being fully compensated for all the carefully chosen risk they assume. They will take no risks by accident and they will be paid the going rate for the risks they do take. But remember, the advocates of MPT sternly warn, this is all any investment advisor can do for you. Forget beating the market. You will be paid the market price of the risk you are accepting. Attempting to go beyond that to a true profit, an "excess return," is hubris and will bring the customary penalties.

Modern portfolio theory in its original form rested on three hypotheses. The curious thing about these three hypotheses is that even most advocates of the theory concede they cannot be proved, in part because they are circular. They can even be hard to distinguish from each other. Moreover, to the extent that they can be empirically tested, the evidence against them has mounted over time. Yet the more vague (and therefore more powerful) ideology created by the formal theory continues to dominate institutional investing in major markets around the world.

The first pillar of modern portfolio theory is the efficient market hypothesis (EMH), which says essentially that modern public securities markets, especially equity markets, are so good at incorporating all available information into security prices that investors who try to beat the market by predicting future prices must fail, at least on average. The great University of Chicago economist Eugene Fama, who articulated the efficient market hypothesis in its modern form in the 1960s, and who has been its greatest advocate, actually did allow for the existence of exceptional investors, the Warren Buffetts of the world. But for ordinary mortals the message of the EMH has been that it doesn't matter how much research you do or how hard you work at it, you can't predict future prices well enough to beat the market.

Is the EMH true? The short answer is that Fama himself said it was not strictly demonstrable. To the extent it can be tested, the evidence for the EMH has looked weaker with every passing decade. Many fewer academics or professionals seem to believe it today than in the 1980s. Market panics naturally tend to deepen this skepticism. Most economists and investment professionals—including your authors—do agree that financial markets have *some* tendency towards efficiency, some proclivity to get prices right, but that was never a controversial point.

In any event, modern portfolio theory requires its practitioners to act "as if" markets are efficient. Which brings us to the next pillar of the MPT: Assuming securities markets get prices right, what are they pricing? Simple. Actually we have already said it: Securities markets price risk. The more risk you take, the more you are paid, which is why stocks pay more than bonds, and stocks from small newish companies pay more than stocks of big established companies.

Wait a second! We said only a few paragraphs ago that the essence of modern portfolio theory is that markets price risk. Now we are calling this one of the hypotheses on which the MPT rests. True. But in order to build a working system to guide investors, the notion of risk needed a mathematical proxy. The first one proposed was the volatility of a security's price—the more a stock or bond price jumped around, the more risky the security. This definition gave birth to the capital assets pricing model or CAPM, the second pillar of modern portfolio theory.

To make a decades' long story short, the CAPM never worked very well. Fama from the beginning pointed out one problem: One could not test any pricing model without assuming market efficiency; and one could not test market efficiency without assuming a pricing model. Another problem was that, after some initially encouraging results, volatility failed as a predictor of returns: more volatile stocks did not reliably pay better than less volatile stocks.

If more volatile stocks do not pay better than less volatile ones, either volatility is not a good proxy for risk, or risk is not the basis of return, or the market is not efficient. Of those three choices, it is the equation of risk with volatility that has been most widely abandoned. Most academics and institutional investors still hold quite fiercely to the underlying notion that risk must be the basis of return. But no attempt to replace the CAPM with a model using a different proxy for risk has attracted much of a following, though quite a number of acronyms have piled up in the alphabetic junkyard.

The final pillar of modern portfolio theory was the assumption that the historic statistical performance of well-defined asset classes would be reasonably stable over time. This notion has long since fallen victim to the "fat tails" problem, the tendency for extreme price movements to happen orders of magnitude more often than statistical models predict (c.f. 1929, 1937, 1974, 1987, 1998, 2000, and 2007–2008). As the statisticians might put it, the "distribution of returns" is not "normal." It does not look just like the bell curve we all carry around in our heads. Again, though most practitioners today believe the historical performance of asset classes has some predictive value, that value is much less strong than it once appeared.

This loss of faith in the predictability of asset classes was actually one of the motives for structured finance. Some asset classes seemed to behave more reliably than others. Default rates for AAA bonds seemed remarkably stable over time. Now it can be mathematically demonstrated (don't worry we aren't going to do that to you) that two portfolios of apparently *very different risk levels*, and thus according to the modern theory *very different return levels* can be made equivalent by varying how much leverage (borrowed money) is used to acquire them. A very stable, safe portfolio of boring old AAA bonds can be magically transformed into the equivalent of a go-go, high-yield, get-rich-quick portfolio of risky high yield bonds simply by borrowing most of the money you use to buy the AAAs.

Why would you do this? There are several possible reasons, but the most important is that despite the founders of the MPT going on about how asset classes perform predictably, most people don't believe that exotic stuff will color inside the lines, and they do believe AAA bonds will. So AAA bonds become a perfect ingredient for a modern portfolio theory approach. Using these nicely predictable pieces of paper, you can create a portfolio of any given risk and return level just by leveraging up. That's a big part of the reason the banks wanted to create AAA paper out of junk.

In any event, of the three pillars of modern portfolio theory, every single one looks shaky today.

We should say that our account of the MPT not only involves some heroic simplifications but would also probably be derided as unfair and inaccurate by a number of the people who were crucial to the MPT's development. Some of those objections would contradict others because modern portfolio theory does not belong to anyone—it evolved through heated arguments among very smart people who often powerfully disagreed with each other over crucial points.

On the other hand, it does not matter much whether we get the MPT precisely right because hardly anyone—precisely—believes it.

But haven't we been saying throughout this book that the ideology represented by the MPT dominates modern investing? Yes, we have and it does, but not in the manner of a scientific theory nor as a mechanical methodology. Modern portfolio theory has

triumphed not as a formula but as a way of thinking about investment, and, above all, as the expression of an ambition.

The MPT defined the ambition of institutional investors and
managers in our time: To treat investment as a quantitative exercise relying on the efficiency of markets and advanced mathematics to eliminate the hazards of human judgment. The market may
not be quite as efficient as Fama once hoped, but most academic
programs take the view that the market is good enough that
trying to beat it is a dangerous thing. Well-defined asset classes
may not be perfectly predictable, but they are widely believed
to be more predictable than individual securities. Nobody really
diversifies into the "world portfolio," but efficient portfolio
diversification is considered a far more important investment tool
than "stock picking." Even in a world in which nobody "really"
believes in the MPT, most professionals and academics alike will
say that proper diversification among well-defined asset classes
is responsible for more than 90 percent of return on securities
investment.

Some of the theory's continued hegemony is surely explained
by professional convenience. By attempting to quantify the source
of investment returns, the pioneers of the MPT transformed investment from a mere praxis into a legitimate branch of economic
science. MPT created a field for which PhDs could be granted
(as Milton Friedman famously resisted doing in the case of Harry
Markowitz, the seminal MPT theorist) and journal articles published. Before MPT, investment theory had been mere reflection
upon experience, a wisdom literature dominated by amateurs like
Benjamin Graham (even if he did teach at Columbia).

MPT has a practical allure for the financial professional also.
A world in which process is everything, original insight is suspect, and the best possible outcome is to earn the same mediocre
returns as everyone else (since excess returns imply exposure to

unacknowledged risk) can be deeply attractive to those trying to support capitalist lifestyles with only bureaucratic talents.

Yet these motives alone seem too thin to explain the continued dominance of a theory that has invited repeated financial market crises over forty years and has garnered tens of thousands of pages of devastating contrary evidence from dissenting researchers.

We believe the most powerful reason for the modern theory's continued power is that it offers an answer both intuitive and seductive to the most important question any investor can ask: For what are investors paid? MPT's answer: For accepting risk.

It may have seemed to those who developed the MPT that the three core hypotheses—the efficient market hypothesis, the CAPM, and the assumption of normal distributions—all supported the central thesis of the MPT: risk determines return. But we suspect the truth was the other way round. It was the enormous intuitive power of equating risk with reward that actually propped up the foundational propositions of MPT.

To see this, we invite you to test the power of this intuition on that most useful of all data-sets, yourself. If you are reading this book, and you have been active or even interested in markets even for a few years, you probably have developed some serious doubts about market efficiency, or any of the mechanical attempts to apply the MPT to actual portfolio construction, not to mention such thoroughly discredited notions as the CAPM and normal distributions. If you have been out of business school and working in financial markets for even a few years, you have probably developed some doubts about what you were taught about how securities markets work and how to make money in them. You probably believe not only that it is possible to beat the market but that you yourself have done so, beaten the pants off it in fact, more than once, and professors be damned. You may even believe that, at the margin, risk can be reduced even while maintaining or even increasing returns, which is only another way of saying you believe you can beat the market—sometimes.

Let's say you believe all that. And yet deep in your trembling heart—at least on the days it trembles—admit it, there is part of you that still believes you are mostly paid for taking risks and that in general the more risks you take, the more you will be paid. If you invest in AAA credits, deep in your heart it is because you believe that the rewards that would flow from the greater risks of investing in stocks are not, for your purposes, worth the risk. If you do invest in stocks it is because, given your purposes and, of course, your "risk profile," you have decided that the risks are justified by the rewards.

Thinking in this way has become second nature to us not only because it is the conventional wisdom but because it seems intuitively correct. Thus the very same contemporary finance textbooks that routinely vent their skepticism about the efficient market hypothesis and the capital assets pricing model (and its successors such as the arbitrage pricing theory) continue to reverence as an indisputable first principle the idea that risk is the basis of return. *Principles of Corporate Finance*, by Brealey, Myers, and Allen, widely used in prestigious university programs, for instance, has this to say: "Few people quarrel with the idea that investors require some extra return for taking on risk. That is why common stocks have given on average a higher return than U.S. Treasury bills. Who would want to invest in risky common stocks if they offered only the *same* expected return as bills?"[21]

Another widely used text, *Analysis for Financial Management*, by Robert C. Higgins, asserts, "Business decisions commonly involve the classic 'eat well–sleep well' dilemma. If you want to eat well, you had best be prepared to take risks in search of higher returns. If you want to sleep well, you will likely have to forgo high returns in search of safety. Seldom will you realize both high returns and safety."[22] *Investment Analysis and Portfolio Management,* by Reilly and Brown, inform us that choosing different securities for a portfolio is essentially a matter of evaluating "the expected risk–return tradeoffs."[23]

This idea that investors are paid for risk is so deeply embedded in the language and metrics of modern finance that even those professionals who reject it can only with the greatest difficulty engage in the public conversation of finance without speaking "as if" it were true. Most true hedge funds are theoretically committed to the idea of earning "superior risk-adjusted returns." Translation: Our goal is to be overpaid for risk, which the modern theory says is impossible. Hedge funds' reason for being is to defy the idea that risk determines investment return. And yet you will shock even most players in the hedge fund world into silence if you deny that risk is *a* dominant source of return. We know, we've tried it. It's difficult to hold conversations even with our own colleagues without implicitly bowing to the idol of risk. We often speak as if success means merely cheating the otherwise sound equation of risk = return, defying nature, and tricking the gods.

Fundamentally the notion that risk drives return is powered not by abstruse financial theory, and certainly not by research, but by a powerful intuition of common sense: "If I wish an investor to put his money in my risky venture, rather than let it sit in his bank, I must pay him more to take that risk, just as if I wish a man to do a risky job, such as walking a tightrope in the circus, I must pay him more than the man who cleans up after the elephants." For finance professionals and academics, however, this idea is not only intuitive, it is seductive. To sum the source of investment return into a quantifiable factor is an idea as alluring as the philosopher's stone and far more plausible.

What do we know? We know investors are paid. That implies they are paid for something. We know investors do incur risk.

Investors invest in the uncertain expectation of making money; usually they make either more or less than they expected. We know also that what investors earn—on average and over time—seems to vary systematically according to what class of assets they invest in.

Over the long term, investing in U.S. stocks, for instance, seems to pay better than investing in high quality U.S. corporate bonds. Investing in the shares of small and obscure companies pays better, on average, than investing in large and well-known companies. And we know that this earnings differential between these very broadly defined asset classes seems to correlate, very roughly, to a specific sort of risk called liquidity risk. Liquidity risk is simply the risk that if you invest $10 in a stock today some of that $10 might not be available as cash tomorrow because the market might have marked your stock down to $9. This may happen, indeed almost always does happen at some point, even if the investment was quite a good one and ends up being worth $20 in a few years.

The probability of an investment-grade corporate bond losing 10 percent of its market value in a single day is much less than the probability that the stock of a typical small-cap start-up company will do the same, but much greater than the probability of a Treasury bill doing so. Since on average and over time investors in small-cap stocks earn much higher returns than investors in AAA corporate bonds, and investors in Treasury bills make still less than investors in AAA corporates, it appears to be true that at least this one type of risk, "liquidity risk" or volatility, does roughly correlate with returns. Or at least it seems to do so when we look at the average performance of large, well-defined asset classes. In other words it seems to work at a high level of abstraction, as long as we ignore almost all the detail that goes on down below where individual investors are making judgments about particular securities.

Thus, if your goal is to give a general account of what investors get paid for—the sort of broad assumption you could plug into an economic model covering securities markets in general, or use as the basis for an academic paper—risk looks like a good, powerfully intuitive, and, above all, seductively simple choice.

The moral intuition that taught the Romans that "fortune favors the brave" is deep and longstanding. Long before the world had anything like modern financial markets as an example, men portrayed courageous defiance of the odds as not only one way to great success but the most noble and admirable way. The moral defenders of capitalism have repeatedly staked the system's legitimacy on the notion that those who take great risks deserve great rewards.

It is this combination of an appealing intuitive notion (investors who risk more must be paid more) with a thrilling moral tale (the capitalist knight wins the kingdom not by counting the beanstalks but by slaying the dragon and leveraging the damsel) that surely explains why the notion of risk as the source of return remains so powerful.

Powerful, persuasive, deeply intuitive but wrong, dangerously and destructively wrong. We believe that the reign of risk is at the root of the repeated crises in modern financial markets and that overthrowing it is the key to successful investment. Far from surrendering to the reign of risk in pursuit of riches, the entrepreneur must rout risk at every turn in order to succeed. The true entrepreneur is not an adventurer but the most prosaic and prudent of men.

We do not propose any mere semantic distinction. We are not playing with words. A man who would prosper in financial markets must first of all free himself from this modern worship of risk. He must work from the exact opposite assumption: risk is not the foundation of profit but its most dreaded enemy. Risk leads not to clarity but to confusion, not to riches but to poverty. To be really successful in the markets, the one thing the investor must do is accurately identify the risks particularly relevant to any investment and go about eliminating them as thoroughly but inexpensively as possible. For eliminating risk always has some cost. Profit is the payment earned by the exercise of judgment to reduce the risk of an enterprise in an economical way. The economical reduction of risk raises the return for any given set of inputs and thus creates new value—the entrepreneurial profit.

Modern financial theory says that—at least in the special case of securities markets—risk drives return. This does not lead the modern investor to take risks heedlessly. Far from being cavalier about risk the great bankers who crashed world credit markets in 2008 were obsessed with risk. They defined investment as the art of structuring, channeling, managing, and massaging risk till they believed they had turned the management of risk into a money machine. They no more embraced risk than men sitting around a campfire embrace the flames. Rather, convinced that risk is the source of wealth they defined their mission as controlling it as men control fire.

They failed catastrophically not because their practice fell short of their theory but because their practice was perfectly informed by their theory, and their theory was wrong. Risk is not the source of wealth in securities markets or anywhere else.

The notion that risk equates with reward is worse than a myth—it is a mass delusion, a mass delusion that in our time has cost investors trillions of dollars that we can measure and the U.S. and global economy probably trillions more that we will never be able to sum. It has lulled an entire generation of financial advisors into complacency about the risks to which they expose their clients. It has led the overwhelming majority of money managers to despair of improving returns by any method other than increased exposure to risk and excused the lethargy of legions of fiduciaries.

This dogma is called "modern" because it represents a radical break with the way both economists and practical investors thought about financial markets previously. The modern theory conceptually severed financial markets from the rest of the economy—what we now call, by virtue of this separation, "the real economy." The universal source of success in the real economy is the application of fresh insight, accumulated skill, and hard work to reduce risks of all sorts, from seven years of drought to stray micro particles on a silicon chip. In the real economy, risk is manifestly not the source of wealth but the great destroyer.

Modern financial theory amounts to the belief that hard work, superior insight, and good judgment—the keys to success in the real economy—are ineffectual for the investor in public financial markets. It tells the investor: hard work and clear thinking doesn't help here, for now you are in a special place where the quaint rules of Main Street do not apply. Here all is mystery; your fate is controlled by forces you can never understand. "But," say the masters of the theory, "We understand. Follow us."

Then one day it becomes clear that the masters do not understand, and panic reigns.

CHAPTER SIX

The Romance of Risk

There were believed to be two kinds of males in American business. There were the true Male Animals, who went into investment banking, hedge funds, arbitrage, real estate development, and other forms of empire building. They were the gamblers, plungers, traders, risk takers. And then there were the passive males who went into commercial banking, where all you did was lend money and sit back and collect interest.

—Tom Wolfe, *A Man in Full*

Who Dares, Wins

—Motto of the British Special Air Service

Before we attempt to overthrow the tyranny of risk in financial theory we must answer an older tale about the role of risk in the real economy, and especially in the life of that greatest of all economic heroes, the entrepreneur. We must first deal with the Romance of Risk. Older than history, this Romance is the essence of every adventure story wherein the hero steps outside the boundaries of his day-to-day existence and confronts the unknown.

Economic life, and particularly entrepreneurship, certainly is an adventure story. Every pursuit of excellence is an adventure. Our objection is not to the real adventure but to the bogus one. Great economic advances usually do require heroic struggles; the men who make those advances are often genuine heroes—even in an important sense, moral heroes. This we celebrate. What we object to is replacing the real heroes with rakes, gamblers, and soldiers of fortune.

Economic theory has generally been uncomfortable with entrepreneurship. A disequilibrating force, entrepreneurship resists modeling. In the late nineteenth and early twentieth century, three great economists—Weber, Schumpeter, and Knight—brought forth inspired accounts of the source of entrepreneurship (Calvinist diligence, inspired innovation, superior judgment). And yet Weber's theory strongly implied that the entrepreneur was dying out, Schumpeter flat out predicted the entrepreneur's demise in a rationalized socialist future (which he hoped never to see), and Knight believed ever-larger firms would dominate the future and obscure entrepreneurial judgments beyond recognition. From the Great Depression through the great malaise of the 1970s, entrepreneurship was increasingly dismissed in a world in which capitalism seemed to have lost its vitality, communism was fondly hoped to be evolving into benign socialist bureaucracy, and conventional opinion fixated on some converged managerial future that would replace both.

Starting roughly in 1980, with the election of Ronald Reagan and the publication of George Gilder's *Wealth and Poverty*, all this changed. Reagan's election and the great boom that followed precipitated a global rehabilitation of capitalism, eventually expanding the ranks of the more or less capitalist world by more than two billion souls, and counting. In a less-celebrated accomplishment, Gilder, a thinker to whom we both owe enormous debts, and with whom Richard has collaborated off and on for many years, changed the way we and just about everyone else talks about capitalism, and thus inevitably the way we think about capitalism.

Adam Smith, precisely by his brilliant unpacking of how markets work, inspired his successors to emphasize the mechanical, fashionably Newtonian aspects of economic growth. As in all Newtonian metaphors, the motive force supposed to drive the mechanics was slighted and simplified, portrayed by Smith as self-interest and by most of his successors as greed. The defenders of capitalism were gripped by this paradox, that one man's greed would provide another man's dinner. Far from shying away from the moral implications, the advocates of capitalism embraced them. What could be better testimony to the power of markets than that they could make greed good?

Gilder shoved aside this imagined "economic man" uniquely motivated by greed and went looking for a real man to put in his place. The motives of Gilder's real man, as with real men everywhere, were not simple and solitary, but manifold and complex. He united the entrepreneur with other creative and driven personalities, men who had achieved great things often at great cost to themselves. For whatever it is that drives a great artist or a great scientist, the one thing that surely cannot explain their greatness, their drive, and extraordinary sacrifices is greed. Surely the struggles of the great entrepreneur look more like the struggles of such men than like the cold calculations of the miser, caged within his counting house, crippled by his lust for gold.

In particular, Gilder argues, the great entrepreneur, like the great artist or the great scientist, creates far more than he consumes, gives more than he will ever take in strictly material terms. Moreover, like the aspiring artist or scientist, the aspiring entrepreneur makes this gift with relatively little hope of return. Just as most artists' work will never hang at the Met and most post-docs will spend their careers contributing but modestly to modest scientific advances, most new businesses fall short of expectations or fail outright. A huge portion of those that succeed do so only because the would-be entrepreneur works longer hours for lower pay than he could have earned by submersing himself in a big company.

So irrational is this behavior in materialist terms, argued Gilder, that not only can it not be called greed, it actually looks like nothing so much as generosity, a gift given perhaps in the hope that it will someday be returned, but with no more surety of return than the gifts offered by a lover. Though often denounced for hyperbole, Gilder's account is surely more accurate and subtle than the unlikely claim of Smith's heirs that the good things of this world are made by sin.

Every great teacher is cursed in his disciples. As with Smith, so with Gilder. Gilder's insight that the work, self-discipline, sacrifice, and, yes, risks incurred by most entrepreneurs were but inadequately compensated by their purely material rewards was quickly debased into rather simplistic hero-worship of the entrepreneur as risk taker. The entrepreneurs themselves, not immune to the attractions of being thought heroes, often echoed this view, as a few scattered examples show:

"I attribute my success to two things. I'm not afraid of taking risks—big risks. In fact, I prefer to take big risks because that's the only way to score big returns."[24]
—David Paschal, president of Paschal Petroleum Inc.

"Entrepreneurs are risk takers, willing to roll the dice with their money or reputation on the line in support of an idea or enterprise."[25]
—Victor Kiam, president and CEO of Remington Products

"If you're not a risk taker, you should get the hell out of business." [26]

—Ray Kroc, McDonald's mastermind

"Every time we've moved ahead in IBM, it was because someone was willing to take a chance . . ."[27]

—Thomas Watson, CEO of IBM

"Risk is the force of entrepreneurship—because where there's risk, there's also a reward . . ."[28]

—Karl D. Bays, chairman of Baxter Travenol Laboratories

We want to believe this. It is a great story. And it has universal appeal. We may not all be able to deceive ourselves into thinking we are brilliant, original thinkers, or that we have accumulated a vast store of experience and insight that might be crucial in launching an enterprise, or that we have the enormous focus and self-discipline common to the great. But we can imagine ourselves brave, or at least foolhardy.

Like Plato's poets, the entrepreneurs turn out to be the worst interpreters of their own works. For this extremely powerful, utterly pervasive idea, from which it seems so hard to free ourselves, is actually an odd and unlikely one. The surprise is not that anyone can manage to reject it but that anyone believes it.

In the real economy we see all the time people being paid for hard work, for perseverance, for insight, and for experience. But it is all but impossible to observe anyone being paid for risk. It is easiest to see this by starting with some extreme cases. There are many great heroes among the great entrepreneurs. It is almost impossible to think of one who got paid for taking risk. The more brilliant the entrepreneur and grand his achievements, the less true it seems. Was Alexander Graham Bell paid for the risk he might not invent the telephone? Nonsense, he was paid for inventing it. Was Edison paid for the risk that he might not invent a light bulb, or for actually inventing it? Henry Ford was not paid for taking the risk that he might not be able to build a car affordable to "any man of good salary"; he was paid for actually doing it. In the extreme case, even insurance companies, as the great Frank Knight pointed out almost a century ago, are paid not for accepting risks but for transforming genuine uncertainty—will I be in an accident?—into statistical predictability—some percentage of drivers will be. Even the flying Wallendas were paid not for their risks but for their skill. Dead acrobats don't get a piece of the gate. Acrobats who risk and fail are less popular than those who succeed despite undertaking greater and greater challenges.

We understand that at first blush this might seem like a trick of rhetoric or equivocation, "mere" semantics. The contrary is closer to the truth. The deeper one looks into these men's lives, the more difficult it is to justify the notion that "risk taking" explains their achievement and rewards. The very notion of risk disappears into incoherence. What are the risks of not inventing a telephone (or a light bulb or an automobile)? Do we mean the odds against doing so? The odds against whom doing so? Anyone, or the men who actually succeeded? If the odds against success are the measure of risk and hence reward, why were these men, who were good candidates to achieve these things and thus took less risk, so well rewarded?

Or by risk do we mean what the entrepreneur had to lose? But the more dramatic the story, the more we see that in their most productive years these men had very little to lose and enjoyed what they were doing far more than most men enjoy their own work. It is at least as true to say that they were "at play" as to say they were "at risk."

Take Ford, whom we just happen to know a bit more about

than we do the others. The harder one looks in the equation of Ford's life for the payoff for risk, the more evanescent it appears. Nor can the risk of failure be in any coherent way related to the fantastic rewards Ford actually earned by success. He certainly took no great financial risk. He started out tinkering with cars as a hobby while serving as chief engineer at Detroit Edison. He built his first several cars while still on Edison's payroll, which means he achieved proof of concept and of his own ability to execute the concept without taking any measurable financial risk. It is not even clear that he had opportunity cost. The challenge invigorated him. It was a hobby. He had already created the Model A before capitalizing Ford Motor, and the original capitalization was not great. His first shareholders could see both the Model A and the fact that Ford had been until recently an accomplished employee of the most famous entrepreneur-inventor in the history of the world.

What were the odds against Ford's success? Should we count up all the crackpots and incompetents in the course of history whoever declared their intention to build a horseless carriage, throw Ford in the mix, and do the long division? If we came up with a thousand crackpots, would that make the odds against Ford a thousand to one? If we came up with ten thousand, would that change the odds?

Of course not. Because Ford was not a crackpot or an incompetent—he was Ford. The risks that Ford would fail cannot be measured against the "odds" that ten thousand others might fail. There is no way to assign a numerical value to Ford's probability of success.

Did it look like a risk to Ford? Did he experience his work as a man shooting craps experiences the roll of the dice? The gambler knows two things for sure: First, everyone else in the game knows the odds—the behavioral properties of dice—as well as he does. Second, he can do nothing (save cheating) to affect the roll. (These are, mutatis mutandis, precisely the driving assumptions of modern portfolio theory.)

Ford's case is opposite the gambler's on both counts. To begin with, as we have seen, in Ford's case there were no odds in a statistical sense, no common knowledge that every player shared. Instead of odds, there was a story about Ford. Many people, including his investors, knew bits of the story. But nobody knew the story as well as Ford, because it was his story.

From his early childhood, Ford was exceptionally good at making things work. His parents raised him as a farmer, but from boyhood he worked in machine shops. From a low-level job at Detroit Edison he worked his way up to become chief engineer. By the time he began tinkering with cars, he had decades of experience successfully addressing engineering problems. If he thought he could build an economically practical car, there was every good reason to believe him. Long before he launched a car company, he confirmed to himself that at a minimum he could build a serviceable car. Unlike the gambler guessing at the odds of rolling seven and knowing just what everyone else knows, Ford knew not just his own abilities, which many people did, but his own determination and level of commitment. Ford had the inside track on Ford.

Aristotle says that a choice is a wish married to the power to effect it. The gambler can only wish for a seven. To a very significant extent, Ford chose to build the first great popular car.

Ford could have been wrong. It was not certain that he could create what became the Model T. Nor was it certain that any of the many other "risky" decisions he made later would turn out right, ultimately transforming Ford Motor into the greatest manufacturing concern in the world. If it would be absurd to call what Ford did gambling, it would be just as absurd to call it a sure thing or claim that Ford "always knew."

Adapting to our own purposes the language of Frank Knight[29]—the great Chicago economist who did more perhaps than any English-speaking economist to clarify these matters—Ford made a "judgment" in the face of "uncertainty." He did not guess and he did not know—he judged. He had a basis for his judgment, but there was some possibility, impossible to quantify, that his judgment was incorrect. One might, using common language, call this possibility a risk, but other terms including "residual uncertainty" would seem just as sensible.

What is perfectly clear is that the process of making the judgments that led to the Model T—a process that effectively comprised all of Ford's life and experience to that point—was overwhelmingly one of reducing the uncertainty, or one might say, of reducing the risk.[30] Ford's judgment was of the sort more likely to increase than reduce wealth, precisely because it involved the cumulative elimination of uncertainty. Can I work a screwdriver? Yes, I can. Can I fix this broken toy? Yes, I can. Can I rise to the top at the local machine shop? Yes, I can. Can I run engineering at Detroit Edison? Yes, I can. Can I build any sort of working car, however awkward? Yes, I can. Can I build a somewhat better one? Yes, I can. Can I convince older men with resources, men like Edison himself, that I am capable? Yes, I can.

Far from profiting by uncertainty or risk, Ford spent decades of his own life, including years of successful practical experimentation specifically on automobiles, reducing the uncertainty confronting his judgment. To say that Ford was paid for taking risk or accepting uncertainty is exactly the opposite of the truth. He was paid for reducing risk, which he did by resolving uncertainties. He was paid for the resolution of uncertainty into productive knowledge. Every day that he worked and read and followed the work of others, he subtracted uncertainty and added to the probability that his vision would prove to be 1.0 correlated with the future.

Understanding an entrepreneur's battle against uncertainty as an unfolding process illuminates another way in which entrepreneurs differ from gamblers. The gambler cannot intervene and nudge dice about to turn up snake eyes. But the entire work of the entrepreneur, once he has set himself a task, is to nudge the dice, shifting the odds in his favor. Judgment, skill, determination, and hard work combine in an interactive process (known technically as life), which is extremely difficult to analyze into separate components. But one thing is perfectly clear. The better Ford's judgment and the more skill, insight, hard work, and determination he brought to bear on the challenge, the less risk remained. And the less the risk, the more likely he was to get paid.

All economic progress looks just like this. Men and societies become richer precisely as they employ insight, skill, and experience, effort and discipline to reduce risk. Facing drought, they irrigate. Facing flood, they drain. Facing seven years of famine, they store. Facing wild beasts, they arm. Facing high but random error rates on nanometer-level chip processes, they build better clean rooms. At every turn of economic life, the reduction of risk is the key to prosperity.

Except in financial markets? Why should it be so?

Well what about Ford's investors? They weren't creative geniuses. They just had money. They were not in as good a position as Ford to assess the likelihood of success and yet they got paid. Why would he give them a large share of his company for their capital if not as a risk premium?

There is no doubt that the investors faced uncertainty, and more than Ford. (This itself should be a hint of the truth since their returns on their greater uncertainty were less than Ford's on his lesser uncertainty.) There is no doubt that they faced some possibility that Ford would fail or that other problems would arise. (Problems did arise, and, for some, there was an angry parting of the ways.) The central fact remains that the investors who got paid, got paid because they had judged rightly that Ford would succeed. They made a judgment under uncertainty. Had their judgment been incorrect, they would not have been paid. Investors are paid for being right, not for the possibility of being wrong.

But couldn't it just have been luck? This is the secret suspicion of the economists and one reason most of them are uncomfortable with the notion of judgment. Financial economics in our time is an overwhelmingly statistical enterprise. But because every judgment, and every judge, is a singular case, statistics and probability are not very useful in assessing judgment. The winner of a coin-flipping contest, if he were fool enough, might go about preening himself on his good judgment in the matter of heads versus tails. Meanwhile, the economists, tearing their hair out in frustration, would be screaming that it was just luck. They would be right. And that is the problem. It is maddeningly possible to confuse good judgment and good luck.

Before economists had statistics, they thrived on imagination. Imagination turns sometimes chaotic experience into stories, which is largely what economics consisted of from at least *The Wealth of Nations* through Marshall's *Principles*. We call stories more true if the characters act according to motivations and with abilities and limitations we recognize from the real world. The extent to which economists' stories seemed consistent with human nature and history used to be the source of their credibility.

Today economists shun imagination and story telling. Not being economists, however, we can imagine Ford's investors very well. And when we imagine them, they don't look at all like men who have won a coin-flipping contest.

Let's do it. Imagine three groups of men. One group is Ford's investors. Another group has shunned Ford and invested all its earthly possessions in any one of a thousand or so crackpot Ford rivals. The third group, declining to make judgments beyond its competence, invests in a diversified portfolio of alleged genius automobile inventors including Ford, Benz, Daimler, and Olds as well as a selection of the crackpots.

Just knowing how they invested tells us who these men are. The ones who invest in a single crackpot are fools, dreamers, and gamblers who feel more certain to the degree they are more ignorant. They die poor. The ones who invest in the diversified portfolio are finance professors, who believe in statistics not judgment. They die with their mortgages paid off. But Ford's investors (we can imagine, though we also know from history) were for the most part men with good judgment and the experience to know they had good judgment. Most were conservative men who made relatively few bold investments during their careers. They made those investments very carefully and were right more often than they were wrong. Most were wealthy men. They got or increased their wealth in large part because they were scrupulous in minimizing uncertainty in their judgments.

In the theory of modern finance an extreme "right tail" event—a hugely profitable trade—implies an extreme "left tail" event to follow. This is because the professors assume that whatever dart-throwing technique produced the extreme right tail hit did so not because the man throwing it had good aim but because he was employing a highly volatile (i.e., highly risky, fraught with uncertainty) strategy. Such a strategy is likely to produce extreme misses as well as extreme hits, which is why the professors expect an extreme left tail event to occur at some point. But life is not like that. In life, men who make one good judgment tend to make more good judgments; men who make one bad judgment tend to make more bad ones. Careful, diligent, and well-prepared men tend to have "good luck" and careless, lazy, and ill-prepared men tend to have "bad luck."

Nevertheless, as Knight concedes, in most cases we would not be able to identify these investors as having good judgment until late in their careers, perhaps not until after they were dead. If we did not know them well, all we would have to go on would be their achievements, the record of previous judgments that had turned out well. The younger the men and the shorter the list of previous judgments, the more likely those apparent good judgments would be mere good luck. With the accretion of accomplishment, or greater knowledge about the men, our confidence might increase. But we would never know for sure. In assessing the quality of their judgment, we would be using our own judgment and using it, as one always uses judgment, under uncertainty. As Knight says, the most important but the most difficult-to-identify ability in business management (or investment) is the ability to judge other men's ability to judge.

Economists dislike the notion of judgment not only because they have no way of verifying that it is not actually luck but also because it limits economics. If good judgment is a driving force of capitalism, then economics as modern professors wish to practice it can't explain capitalism. Like all social science, economics seeks to explain a category of human activity according to a set of rules of sufficiently general application in order to be able to predict future human behavior under circumstances previously described by the rules. Economics wants to be physics.

Economists, like physicists, work with models. Both understand those models to be abstractions from reality not mirrors of it. But from where do these abstractions come? From groups of similar instances. The groups may be small—like two cannon balls of different sizes dropped from the leaning Tower of Pisa—but they must be large enough to make it possible to extract the general principle. Selecting the group is crucial to identifying the principle, which is why science is so keen on "control groups."

Judgments cannot be sorted into scientifically useful groups. Even the various judgments of a single person, like one of Ford's investors, cannot be turned into a statistical group for the purpose of assessing with anything like scientific accuracy the quality of his future judgment. The gap between consciousnesses makes judgments forever incomparable. We can make a commonsense judgment of our own that one who has judged well in the past will judge well in the future. But that is not science.

The two great tools of the intellect are conception and judgment. Concepts arise from what things have in common. Judgment pertains to the irreducible differences between things, to what is unique about them. Conceptual propositions arise from abstraction and definition and for that reason are always demonstrably true or false. I give you a definition of man and then you tell me if Socrates is one. If you have applied the definition correctly I must agree. A teacher shows a child a red ball, a red mailbox, and a red raincoat, then asks what color the stop sign is.

Logic and abstraction can get us thus far but cannot give us proof, for instance, that Socrates or the stop sign actually exists, for the simple reason that existence is not common. There may be two otherwise identical red balls. But they are not the same ball because there are *two* of them. The existence of each is unique, even if nothing else about them is unique. If we know that one is called red, from that we can say whether the other is red. But the existence of one says nothing about the existence of the other. Socrates is a man, but he is neither any man nor every man. To say whether Socrates actually exists, we need to make a judgment not about men but about Socrates, about one single alleged man.

I can have as perfect an idea of a red ball that does not exist as I can of one that does exist. Nothing I can abstract or define will prove that the ball I am thinking of exists. In two thousand five hundred years of trying, no philosopher has ever come up with a way to prove analytically that something exists in the same sense that he can prove Socrates is a man or that two plus two is four. I must judge for myself that one ball exists and the other does not. And I can never be sure in the same way I can about conceptual knowledge. Confronting existence, we are alone (except for God, who, to keep us from being slaves, refuses to judge for us). To affirm existence is to make a judgment, and all judgments are ultimately solitary acts.

The assertion of existence, for which philosophers have long used the term "judgment," is not the only sort of judgment. But this philosophical use does catch exactly the common sense of the word. The assertion that something exists has exactly the three qualities we observe in any judgment. Judgment is always subjective, a personal affirmation. No judge, no judgment. Judgment is always about what is particular rather than common (even though common knowledge may be crucial to good judgment). And precisely because judgment is always particular, it is always made in the face of some uncertainty. No uncertainty, no need for judgment. Logic can be "compelling." But judgments are not like that. We don't give in to them, we make them.

We feel perfectly confident in saying that men who exercise good judgment are more likely to prosper in this world than men who do not. We feel perfectly confident in saying that societies in which capital tends to flow toward men who exercise good judgment will tend to be more prosperous than societies that impede this flow.

We are perfectly confident of all this. But now try to turn this story into a testable hypothesis, much less a theory or a "law." How would we state it? "Good judgments are better than bad judgments." "Good judgments lead to prosperity." That gets us nowhere. To make economics out of this, we would need a reasonably clear definition of good judgment, preferably one we could express mathematically. And then we would need to be able to test it statistically.

Economists like thinking about markets because they have been able to give reasonably precise definitions of things like supply and demand and develop a mathematics expressing the relationships between them. The invention of supply and demand curves didn't end the argument about markets; in some ways it intensified it. And no one believes that the resulting models are anything but an approximation. Nevertheless we can have very powerful working theories of supply and demand precisely because they are abstractions: for the purposes of the models any demand or supply can be portrayed as being much like another. That commonality is the thing that is abstracted, the concept. The model is about the commonality. The unique qualities of individual examples are precisely what don't matter to the model. So trivial for the purposes of these models are the actual qualities of actual things demanded and supplied that economists subsume them in a word expressing their triviality: *widgets*.

Can anyone imagine developing a model of good judgment in the way we have models of demand and supply? Can one imagine thinking usefully about a judgment without contemplating its object, or for that matter its subject? Can one think usefully about judgments by reducing them to widgets? Of course not. This resistance to abstraction makes judgment impossible to model. And yet good judgment is so much the source of wealth that in its absence the most fabulous riches are water poured out on sand.

CHAPTER SEVEN

What Professors Do

The claim that financial markets pay investors who hold appropriately diversified portfolios in proportion to the risks of such portfolios requires in turn the claim that financial markets are efficient, that they get prices right. In order to pay investors in proportion to the risks they take, the market must price risk correctly. Without efficient markets it would make no sense to claim that markets price anything correctly. For risk to determine investment return, the efficient market hypothesis must be true. Even more important, for our purposes, the history of the debate over the efficient market hypothesis offers powerful insights into the manner of thought that drives modern investment theory and which drove the mortgage crisis.

Fifty years ago, the academic study of finance barely touched on portfolio management or investment in public securities markets. Modern portfolio theory changed that. As academic economists moved deeper and deeper into the practical world of securities investment, they followed the natural lines of their discipline and exalted the importance of market machinery over the disruptive, disequilibrating, and unquantifiable notions of entrepreneurship and human judgment. This glorification of market mechanics over human judgment was far more crucial to the mortgage crisis than any strict application of modern portfolio theory or literal belief in the efficient market hypothesis.

Eugene Fama, the great University of Chicago economist who first defined the efficient market hypothesis, explained the term this way:

"In general terms the ideal is a market in which prices provide accurate signals . . . [such that] investors can choose among the securities . . . under the assumption that security prices at any time 'fully reflect' all available information. A market in which prices always 'fully reflect' available information is called 'efficient.'"[31]

In classical theory the sign of a perfect market is the absence of true profit after everyone including investors is paid the market rate for their inputs. In securities markets making a true profit means "beating the market": earning above-average returns after accounting for all costs.[32] For this reason, from the very beginning, attempts to statistically test whether investors can beat the market have dominated the debate over the efficient market hypothesis.

This is certainly not the only way one could go at the question. The debate could have proceeded descriptively. Economists could have proceeded by asking, "What does the interaction of theory and experience tell us a relatively efficient market should look like?" They might even have asked, "When Smith and the others were formulating classical theory what did they observe in the world that made them think that some markets were better at setting prices than others?" Then, looking at securities markets, they could have asked themselves, "Do securities markets look like our general picture of efficient markets? When we describe the operation of public securities markets is our description close to a persuasive picture of a market under perfect competition?"

That is not what happened at all. On both sides, the argument over efficiency has proceeded with remarkably little theory, remarkably little "story telling about markets." For some forty years the debate has consisted almost entirely of the two sides hurling statistics at each other.

The first great debate was over what Fama dubbed the "weak form" of the EMH. Fama helped pay his way through college working for one of his professors who wrote an investment newsletter. The professor claimed to be able to predict future stock prices simply by looking at trends in past prices. This is the realm of "technical analysis"—the making of charts, with "heads" and "shoulders," bottoms and tops, "support levels" and "ceilings," all that sort of thing. Fama became convinced that his employer was a humbug. In the effort to prove the point, he migrated from a prospective career professing French literature to become one of the great economists of our time.

The weak form of the efficient market hypothesis says simply that the work of Fama's erstwhile employer and all other technical analysts is bunk. The weak form says nothing about the work of "fundamental" analysts who study financial statements and visit companies and interview customers to decide which widget-makers' shares are worth more and which less. (The idea that fundamental analysis is bunk is the "strong" form of the EMH and would come later.)

The very next price change in a publicly traded stock will be statistically indistinguishable from a random change, declares the weak form of the EMH. It is impossible to predict from a stock's last five or ten or ten thousand price changes whether its next move will be up or down, big or small. Trying to draw a chart of future stock prices from a chart of past prices is a fool's errand.

Note that if securities markets are doing a good job of setting prices, as the efficient market hypothesis claims, then those prices are not actually random. Quite the opposite. In an efficient market, prices are fully "determined" by the flow of information that the market is processing. "Statistically random" as we are using it here simply means unpredictable by the observer, given the limited information (past prices) available to him.

Fama and others came up with two sorts of tests to try out this proposition. One was to test for "serial independence"—the idea that there is no statistically significant relationship between one price move and the next. The research on this point is now voluminous, but the upshot has not changed much since Fama's 1970 paper: this is almost but not quite true. On average, the *direction* of a stock's next move looks almost random. The *size* of the next price move looks somewhat less random; large moves have a noticeable tendency to follow large moves and small moves to follow small.

However, as Fama himself pointed out early on, demonstrating that share prices are "serially independent," or almost so, does not in itself prove whether technical analysis can produce a profit, the real test of efficiency. For that, we must test actual trading rules that technical traders use and claim to find profitable.

Others had done some work along these lines and found slight positive returns from some trading rules, which might suggest technical analysis was not all bunk. But the profits from such rules were not big enough to overcome the high trading costs the rules required. Fama's own research actually looked more encouraging for the chart makers: "In particular the results for very small filters . . . indicate it is possible to devise trading schemes based on very short term . . . price swings that will on average outperform buy and hold. [Buy and hold was Fama's proxy for "the market gets it right."] The average profits on individual transactions from such schemes are miniscule, but they generate transactions so frequently that over longer periods and ignoring commissions they outperform buy and hold by a substantial margin."[33] Still, he concluded, "departures from the strict implications of the efficient markets model" are so small "that it hardly seems justified to use them to declare the market inefficient."[34] Twenty years later in another review of the evidence he drew essentially the same conclusion: past price moves can be used to predict only "a small part of the variance of returns."[35]

On one level this is a perfectly reasonable conclusion. Most professional practitioners who make some use of technical analysis, as we do, would probably agree: on average it can be used to predict only a small portion of the market's future behavior, especially when applied to the broad market over long periods of time.

What nearly all the academic research on both sides necessarily missed, however, was that technical analysis can be a very powerful—and profitable—predictor of prices over short time periods in narrow segments of the market. The reason the professors missed this is far more important than the fact that they missed it. This failure was not a "mistake." It was not a phenomenon the professors "should have" seen, given their approach to the problem. They missed it not because they did their research badly but because they did it well; not because they were sloppy but because they were scrupulous. Missing the reality was an inevitable consequence of basic standards of scientific research as adopted by the social sciences in pursuit of intellectual rigor. They were required by their own protocols to exclude the very force they were investigating—the power of human judgment to create entrepreneurial profits.

Importing scientific standards into economics has several implications including rigorous exclusion of observer bias and the requirement that results must be reproducible by other researchers. In the efficiency debate, these standards played out in several ways. One was the requirement that any phenomenon suggesting inefficiency, any "anomaly" observed for one time period, must be observable in others—or even better, in all time periods for which we have good data. Moreover, these time periods must be arbitrarily defined before the data is examined. They should be reasonably long (five years would be short). And we should be able to observe the anomaly again "out of sample," i.e., in some other arbitrarily defined time period. Suppose in a ten-year study a researcher observed evidence that past prices predicted future prices for the first seven months, not in the next twelve months, then saw some positive evidence again for thirteen more months, after which it did not appear again for six months, and so on. None of those results would be considered persuasive scientifically. The periods are not only short but more importantly the researcher failed to arbitrarily define them beforehand. The proper scientific result would be that of the whole ten years, a reasonably long, predefined block of time. If an academic studied ten years of prices, and then reported evidence only from those years supporting his conclusions, he would be dismissed as a fraud. If, intrigued by a few months in which he had observed strong evidence of a phenom-enon, a researcher developed a hypothesis about why the phenom-enon appeared during those months, this work would be suspect, inspired as it was by "data mining"—searching first for a result and then proposing a hypothesis supposedly supported by it.

Similarly, academic economists consider results valid only if they apply across an entire market segment previously defined in some nonbiased way. They can look for anomalies across the S&P 500, or across all NYSE stocks, or the NASDAQ, or even the Dow, or randomized portions of any of these. For certain pur-poses, they might even look for trends in some other easily for-malized categories such as large-cap stocks or small-cap stocks. But if a researcher looking for evidence that past prices predicted future prices searched historical data on the S&P 500 and then presented only the evidence from the 43 stocks that seemed to support his conclusion, excluding evidence from the other 457, he would be laughed out of the university.

And yet this is exactly what adroit market practitioners do. We assume that potentially profitable anomalies appear and disappear as market conditions change. We assume that such anomalies are almost certain to be more powerful and profitable for some sets of securities than for others. We look into the nooks and crannies of the market for trends that we can exploit profitably with some securities for now. We hypothesize strategies that seem suited to current market conditions, test them, and then trade on promising results. When we build quantitative tools, our goal is not to find algorithms that work for all eternity across any arbitrarily defined class of securities. We look for tools that deliver very strong results over time periods biased to the near term. And in building the universe of securities to which to apply the algorithm, we do not choose some neutrally defined class that would please an academic such as every stock in the S&P or every large cap. We select a subset of securities with favorable characteristics that make them good candidates for the algorithm. We "back-test" to see if they behave. Once we go live, we monitor the universe, tossing securities whose behavior no longer seems to be well predicted by the algorithm and adding others that seem promising.

From the late 1990s through roughly 2002, U.S. equity prices were unusually volatile. So we and other practitioners launched strategies that worked well under conditions of high volatility. One we used at the time was "pair-based short-term mean reversion." Translation: we match pairs of fundamentally similar stocks, whose prices normally tend to move up or down together (e.g., Exxon and Mobil). During times of high volatility, however, such customary correlations may break down for no apparent economic reason. An unusual gap will open up between the prices of the pair. If there really is no economic reason for the gap, it tends to close fairly soon (because markets do have *some* tendency to efficiency). We buy the loser and short the gainer when the gap opens and make money when the gap closes.

For half a decade or so, this was an easy way to make money. Then two things happened. Lots of traders and lots of money poured into the strategy, and record-high volatility became record-low volatility. All of a sudden there were fewer opportunities (gaps) and more people chasing them. The strategy stopped working. So over time we and most of our competitors moved capital out of this strategy and into others. That's how we make a living.

That good half-decade makes an unlikely subject of an academic paper. To prove this strategy's validity, a researcher would need an arbitrarily defined time sample. An academic study running from 1999, when we started using this strategy, to 2003, when we started reducing our allocation to it, would look suspiciously contrived. And then having done his study for one arbitrarily defined period, the academic would need an "out of sample" test as well. In other words, in order to prove that the strategy was the real thing and not luck, an academic researcher must test it under conditions that make it bound to fail. When it does fail, the academic will dismiss the technique as a trader's delusion. The trader's conclusion is that the strategy works when conditions are favorable.

Nor is this the only "bias" we practitioners employ in our "studies." To get pair trading to work, for instance, one must pick the right stocks. In this strategy we do not trade every stock, or even every conceivable pair of stocks on the NYSE, or in the S&P 500. We don't trade every large-cap pair or every pair within any neutral "unbiased" set that would satisfy academic or scientific requirements. We select a small subset of stock pairs (called the trading "universe") with especially favorable characteristics. We "back-test" promising pairs from that universe to see if they behave. Once we go live, we monitor pairs and sectors for signs that the relationship is no longer working. From time to time we drop pairs that no longer work and add pairs that seem promising.

Just imagine the reception a graduate student would receive if he explained to his thesis advisor that from time to time he excluded experimental subjects that were not exhibiting the behavior he was trying to prove and added new ones that hadn't looked promising earlier but now were cooperating in proving his thesis! We do it every day.

But wait, it gets worse. Our sins mount yet higher! Even though this is a largely quantitative statistical strategy, in our version success requires qualitative intervention. We choose pairs in part because of a qualitative judgment that their history of correlation makes sense rather than being the result of chance or fleeting circumstances. For instance we don't trade technology stocks in this strategy because the pace of innovation in hi-tech makes it hard to judge whether two technology companies really are fundamentally similar or will remain so. Also, when a price gap opens, before we make the trade we double check to make sure there has been no fundamental development that could be responsible, reducing the likelihood of short-term mean-reversion. Virtually all our quantitative strategies include a qualitative element—human beings making subjective human judgments. Even more purely quantitative firms that rely less on human judgment than we do use lots of computer "judgment," allowing the machines to adjust the algorithm to evolving market conditions.

Again, just imagine the reaction if an academic researcher, on the basis of such qualitative judgments, tossed from his sample securities that tended to disprove his thesis, while including those that tended to prove it. Even if he were performing a real-time study, less subject to systematic bias, and was able to demonstrate the success of his trading system, his reliance on his own qualitative judgment would mean the experiment would not be reproducible.

Judgment implies consciousness; between any two consciousnesses, there is always an unbridgeable gap. The element of judgment would always leave open the possibility that the researchers' results were driven by luck, which is precisely how modern portfolio theory accounts for investors who beat the market.

To the practitioner, the academic who proclaims some strategy only minimally useful "on average" is like the proverbial economist with his head in the oven and his feet in the icebox who finds the temperature, on average, comfortable. This is not because the academics are fools or the practitioners knaves but because the two groups are pursuing incompatible goals. The practices of one group cannot be measured by the standards of the other. No academically reputable test can reproduce the behavior of any adept practitioner, unless the practitioner himself is using an extremely formalized and inflexible strategy (always buy small caps; always buy cheap stocks). That inflexibility will cost his investors a great deal of money during years the strategy does not fit market conditions.

The academic debate on market efficiency shows essentially no consciousness of this problem. On both sides the participants in the argument are obsessed with excluding "bias." But what professors call bias, practitioners call "thinking." Judgment cannot be evaluated scientifically precisely because, in some irreducible respect, every judgment is sui generis; no judgment is ever reproducible.

Judgments cannot be specified before the "experiment" because they are reactions to events that occur after the experiment has commenced. Inevitably judgments appear as instances of bias or ad hoc manipulation of the data. This appearance is perfectly accurate. Judgments are ad hoc. The most particular function of a judge in a courtroom is to manage ad hoc events into the formal system known as law.

Because the question of market efficiency is ultimately about the possibility of profit in actual financial markets at particular times under particular circumstances, it is impossible to settle the question using primarily formal techniques that strip away information and insight the practitioner regards as essential. It is impossible to address the question of whether good judgment can produce excess returns through research methods that exclude the possibility of judgment.

The apparent orderliness of any system depends on the level of abstraction at which the observer is operating. For the purposes of an architectural model of a skyscraper, it would not matter that some of the bricks in the real skyscraper had tiny irregularities. The architect need not make a judgment about every brick. But if we were using bricks to polish a high-precision surface, an irregularity would be a disaster.

The higher the level of abstraction from which we view the market, the more orderly it appears. Over the long haul—since the 1920s by some measures, longer by others—U.S. stock markets have paid about 7 percent a year adjusted for inflation, AAA bonds about 2 percent, and so forth. Seen from that perspective the market is calmly omniscient, certainly more so than any observer. If we could make only one investment decision every hundred years, the only correct course would be to diversify as broadly as possible and hope that very long-term trends would continue. We could not reliably outthink the market on a hundred-year scale. On the other hand there have been periods of longer than a decade for which investing in the stock market in expectation of a 7 percent real return turned out to be a devastating mistake. It took the market twenty-five years to regain its levels of 1929.

The inclination of the academic student of finance is to raise the level of abstraction sufficiently high to generate general, testable, and reproducible rules about the market's behavior. The academic generally does not say "look at this brick" except by way of making a general statement about all bricks or a class of bricks. The academic works with concepts not cases; with rules, not exceptions; with continuity not disruption; with markets not entrepreneurs.

Similarly, very large institutional investors, impelled by the need to invest tens or hundreds of billions, tend naturally to operate at high levels of abstraction. Smaller, more flexible investors (in our day represented largely by hedge funds) take advantage of the tendency of large investors to shed detail. We operate "underneath" the large-scale models used by institutions, at a lower level of abstraction. The institutional investor buys bricks by the truckload and values each the same—he is building a skyscraper. We paw through each individual brick looking for one of curious shape that enhances its value. The bank dumps thousands of pennies into a sorting machine that spits out rolls. We turn over each penny looking for a "1914 d."

This works for us even when the institutional investor is behaving perfectly sensibly. Most of the time the institution is right to ignore the individual pennies. Even a '14 d is worth only about a hundred bucks. Should the bank complicate its daily business by looking at every penny? But for us it makes sense: it's our business and the scale on which we operate. The institutional investors are effectively outsourcing to hedge funds (among others) the job of finding small inefficiencies in the market and correcting them— for which we make a profit.

For a large buyer, a few bad apples in the barrel is neither an embarrassment nor a disaster. That's what diversification is for, and it always leaves a little value on the table for others to scoop up. The great danger is to forget the natural risks of operating at a higher level of abstraction and forgo the precautions necessary to do so. It is not important for the architect to check every brick. It is essential to spot-check and employ other safeguards so that he knows he has not used so many substandard bricks as to threaten the building. The great danger is to assume that because one brick wall looks very much like another from ten thousand feet, that the bricks no longer matter. Modern portfolio theory teaches investors not to think about the bricks at all.

So you build the building, rent every floor. And at ten o'clock Monday morning, with the offices packed, you get the call. Some of the bricks are bad. Not sure how many, really—no way to tell. But maybe too many. Maybe the building could fall. Or maybe not.

Panic, anyone?

CHAPTER EIGHT

Dumb Money Rules

By itself, the "weak form" of EMH, which merely said that technical analysis does not work, was not sufficient to create a new ideology of finance. It was not the rejection of technical analysis that overthrew the old paradigm. The old paradigm had already soundly rejected it. Neither Benjamin Graham nor any other important wise man of the old school had any use for technical analysis.[36] Graham thought "Mr. Market," as he called it, insane. He certainly was not going to consult past series of insane prices in order to predict future series of insane prices. Had technical analysis simply been outlawed by an act of Congress in, say, 1960, the world barely would have noticed.

The real argument about the efficient market hypothesis is not about whether the fractional predictability that academic statisticians detect over long series of market prices should be considered a glass half full or half empty. The real argument can be reduced to a single question: "Is the market ruled by the smart money or by the dumb money?" Can groups of inept investors making systematic errors about prices create large and reasonably durable gaps between value and price that smart investors can take advantage of? Can prices be wrong enough long enough that it makes sense to adopt a strategy of searching for such mispricings through fundamental analysis of company value, rather than simply buying an efficiently diversified portfolio? Or is the smart money so dominant that in effect all the smart investors working in competition make it impossible for any of them to make above-average returns? Is the smart money creating the market of perfect competition and no profit?

By dumb money we don't mean any individual investor making one mistake. By smart money we don't mean any one investor having an occasional profitable insight. Rather the efficient market theory presumes that whenever a dumb investor misprices a security the smart money rushes so rapidly to take advantage of that mistake that the security is almost immediately and correctly repriced. According to the EMH priesthood this process is on average so swift that it is all but impossible to beat the market, on average and over time, through a strategy of searching out mispricings. For any given transaction, the value hunter may be successful. But the market is dominated by lots and lots of smart investors ever alert to mispricings and eager to benefit from them. Moreover, prices in liquid markets typically move as a function of hundreds or thousands or even tens of thousands of closely bid transactions over the course of a day, militating against the opening of large gaps and assuring that small gaps will close quickly. On average then, even the smart investor particularly focused on value is likely to marginally overpay almost as often as he marginally underpays. After transaction costs and adjusting for risk, the game will not be worth the candle.

We did some complaining last chapter about the paucity of useful theorizing about markets undergirding the EMH. But on the question of whether smart money rules the market, there is a little bit of theory. It is called the "Friedman argument," in honor of Milton Friedman who is generally credited with formulating it. It goes like this: Assume financial markets start out with a normal distribution of smart and dumb investors, each with about the same capital to work with. Over time the dumb investors make bad choices, buying high and selling low. Inevitably their capital shrinks. At the same time the smart investors are buying low and selling high. Inevitably their capital grows. Soon smart investors control overwhelmingly more capital than dumb investors. Many dumb investors are driven out of the market entirely. The remaining dumb investors may continue to make mistakes. But with their now paltry purses, their influence on price is minimal. The remaining minor mispricings are arbitraged away faster and faster at less and less profit: the market achieves efficiency.

Notice something very important about this argument. The efficient market therein described is not metaphor, much less magic. It is not run by an invisible hand. It depends on the actual abilities of the actual players in actual financial markets. Though stated theoretically, it depends on the very empirical claim that smart players have a lot more money and market power than dumb players. If the two groups, smart and dumb, were even reasonably closely matched, then dumb money would have a larger and more durable impact on prices than contemplated by the EMH. Mispricings would be larger than predicted and endure for longer. Trying to beat the market by chasing mispricings would become a more credible strategy.

Though "the Friedman argument" in itself is certainly a piece of theory, in practice the argument over whether smart money actually dominates the market, like the argument over technical analysis, has been overwhelmingly empirical and statistical. Starting with the work of Jack Treynor and Michael Jensen in the 1960s there has been a series of research papers on the point.[37] Most of these papers study the performance of professional money managers, usually mutual fund managers because the data on their performance is a matter of public record. The efficient market advocates argue that if there is any class of investors who should be able to outsmart the market, it should be these professionals. Yet study after study has shown that they don't. On average, mutual fund managers consistently fail to outperform the market and usually underperform after fees and transaction costs are taken into account.

Of course every year a lot of managers do beat the market by wide margins. But this proves nothing, because as the efficient market guys point out, they don't do it consistently. With extremely rare exceptions, the top fund managers in one year are as likely as any to be among the worst the following year. Only a sprinkling of legendary managers, such as Peter Lynch in the 1980s, have put together long streaks of top performance. And the ranks of these legendary managers are so thin that even their astounding winning streaks are consistent with dumb luck—like the guy who wins the coin-flipping contest. Lynch flipped heads ten times in a row. Based solely on that information, he could be the village idiot.

The natural conclusion: if even professional money managers, the smartest money in the market, can't consistently beat the market then obviously no one can. The market is collectively smarter than all the smart money. Paradoxically, the smart guys can't outsmart the market, precisely because they do their work of erasing even tiny market efficiencies so well. The "Friedman argument" is vindicated.

This assumes, however, that on average mutual fund managers are actually "smart money." But what if they aren't? What if on average mutual fund managers are dumb? What if stocks particularly favored by mutual funds tend to underperform? What if the stocks they ignore tend to overperform? What if you could make money just by doing exactly the opposite of what mutual fund managers do?

The implications would be enormous. For one thing, one of

the more persuasive empirical proofs of the efficient market theory would be upset. And that's not all. The importance of these supposedly smart money managers to efficient markets goes far beyond their role in one proof for the theory. In efficient market theory, those smart money managers are the crucial mechanism of efficiency. They don't just prove efficiency; they are supposedly its source. If mutual fund money is actually dumb, then given the huge capitalization of those funds, it would be very hard for stock markets to be dominated by smart money. If mutual fund money is dumb, then the stock market is probably not so bright either.

In 2005, a remarkable paper was published by two scholars, Professor Owen Lamont, of the Yale School of Management and the National Bureau of Economic Research, and Andrea Frazzini, a recent Yale PhD in economics.[38] Yale's business school is a hotbed of research in "behavioral finance." (Andy is a financial supporter of Yale's behavioral finance program.) Behavioral finance explores the nexus of finance and psychology to understand why both people and markets seem frequently to behave in economically irrational ways.

At a conference introducing their paper, "Dumb Money: Mutual Fund Flows and the Cross-Section of Stock Returns," Professor Lamont began by raising an intriguing question. Why should we assume that mutual funds are smart money? It is true that mutual fund managers are mostly highly educated professionals who know their way around financial filings, put a lot of time and effort into choosing the securities for their portfolio, and have access not only to all the best research but usually to the companies themselves. Whether security analysis is an art or a science, surely they are as good as any artists or scientists around. But, Lamont asked, do all these qualifications—or even some managers' very real abilities—actually matter?

Well, what could be more important? Lamont's answer: "their

customers." People who put money in mutual funds do so for the avowed reason that they lack the skill, the inclination, or the time to manage their investments for themselves. They are by definition "dumb" or at best "random" money. Acting usually on the basis of very little information, they give their money to relative strangers who claim, contrary to the available evidence, to be able to deliver better returns than the investors could get themselves by throwing darts at stock tables.

Despite the considerable evidence that the past performance of mutual fund managers is no guarantee of future performance, many mutual fund investors clearly believe the opposite. Considerable research shows that mutual fund investors do choose funds based on recent past performance. Investors flock to hot funds. They also favor funds with names suggesting currently fashionable investment styles and funds that do lots of advertising. Mutual fund investors tend to go with the crowd and hop on the bandwagon.

So, customers and capital tend to flow to recently successful mutual managers. But it is just these recently successful managers who, according to voluminous research, are quite likely to be heading for a bad year. Rather than being re-sorted to the consistently skillful, capital is re-sorted to managers more likely to be headed for a crack-up.

Still, once these managers get the money, aren't they likely to handle it better than their investors would have? Maybe. But, Lamont warns us, keep in mind how investors choose a particular fund in the first place. Yes, recent performance tends to be a powerful factor, but that performance usually is part of a "story" about the fund's investment principles and style. Maybe the fund had great performance last year on tech stocks. Maybe the manager is smart as a whip and really believes that techs are played out. Maybe he wishes he could stray. In practice, though, a manager who abandons last year's successful strategy is setting himself up for major outflows of capital and diminished fees and profits. If he is part of a group and has a boss, he may find himself out of a job.

In short, as Lamont puts it, it is very hard for a mutual fund manager to be smarter than his customers. His customers give him their money expecting him to do what he did last year, which may be a very dumb thing to do this year.

It's a nice argument, apparently insightful about the way the world works, clever in the way that Friedman's is clever. But is it true? That's what Lamont along with Andrea Frazzini set out to determine.

The precise question Lamont and Frazzini proposed for investigation was whether investor sentiment (as measured by the mutual funds to which investors are shifting their money) correlates with investment returns. If investors on average are good at picking mutual funds, then funds experiencing large capital inflows should do well compared to the average, as should the stocks in which those funds are especially heavily invested. But if investors are bad at picking funds, then funds receiving lots of new capital should do relatively poorly, as should the stocks in which those funds are concentrated. If investors consistently favor funds that are about to do badly, then contrary to the Friedman argument they massively shift capital away from the smart money coalition and over to the forces of the stupid.

The two scholars studied twenty-five years' worth of investment flows into and out of hundreds of mutual funds and the thousands of stocks in which those funds invested. They also studied the performance of both the funds and the individual stocks to see whether popular funds into which investors were pouring money (and the stocks those funds invested in) did better or worse than unpopular funds from which investors were withdrawing money (and the stocks those funds invested in). They were able to draw some powerful conclusions. In short: the customer is always wrong.

First and foremost, investors who actively reallocate between mutual funds are in fact dumb money. Chasing hot funds is a big mistake, at least the way most investors do it. Previous researchers had noted, and Lamont and Frazzini confirmed, that an investor who hops on and off the bandwagon at just the right interval can do well. But the right interval is very short. Investors who reallocate their money every quarter to funds from among the top performers for the immediate previous quarter will enjoy higher returns.

Most investors don't do that. They wait too long. They switch money out of funds that have disappointed for a year or more and into funds that have performed well for a year or more. These funds, the funds that are the most popular with investors, the funds that receive the largest share of capital flows, then quickly start to underperform. And the stocks that are especially favored by fashionable mutual funds, the ones that get most of the new money from investors, on average perform badly for any time horizon longer than three months. Over three years, on average, the top 20 percent of stocks, measured by how much new investment they got from mutual funds, underperformed stocks that got the least new investment by about 8 percentage points per year. If fashionable stocks went up 7 percent in a year, on average unfashionable stocks would be up 15 percent per year. Similarly, the most fashionable mutual funds underperformed the least fashionable by about 3.6 percentage points a year.

The "dumb money" effect shows up as stronger or weaker depending on how the authors control for other possible explanatory factors. But for large funds and when measuring performance over a three-year horizon, it never disappears.

This should not have been much of a surprise. Lamont and Frazzini's research echoes two of the most well-established tendencies of securities markets: the "value" effect and the "reversal" effect. The value effect says that cheap stocks—stocks that investors have been selling—on average produce higher returns than expensive or "growth" stocks. Reversal says that a group of stocks that have had very low returns over some previous mid- to long-term period, such as three years, will in the next few years outperform stocks that yielded very high returns in the past period. Just think "first shall be last and last shall be first" and you've got it.

Take a value stock (or a loser stock) and watch it overperform for several years. Presto! Now it's a growth stock or a winner stock and ready for a fall. That's just when mutual fund investors tend to buy it, by switching to the funds that rode up with it over the past few years.

Not surprisingly dumb money seems to get even dumber in times of extreme behavior and trendiness: bubbles and busts. Although the dumb money effect was detectable for 16 out of the twenty years in the sample, it was most pronounced for the bubble years from 1998 through 2002. Those four years alone accounted for about two-thirds of the wealth destruction experienced during the whole twenty years by investors chasing hot mutual funds.

Finally, if mutual fund investors are dumb, who is smart? Mostly the companies selling their stock to overeager investors. Companies that find their stocks in fashion with mutual fund managers tend to issue a lot more new stock than companies whose stocks are out of fashion. In effect the managers of these firms, being far better informed about their own companies' real prospects than the mutual-fund-buying public, are selling high so as to raise capital cheaply from the dumb money that rules the market. Again, this should be no surprise. Substantial research has long shown that firms that issue new stock tend to underperform the market in subsequent years while those who buy back their own stock tend to overperform.

What does it all mean? Simple: mutual fund money—long assumed to be smart money, run by professional managers who help arbitrage away mispricings—is, on average, dumb money. The most popular mutual funds, the ones attracting the most money at any given moment, the ones whose influence in the market is growing, are not healing mispricings; they are creating them. Rather than arbitraging away price anomalies, the behavior of the most fashionable mutual funds seems to be partly responsible for creating some of the most well-documented stock market anomalies, including the value effect and the reversal effect, by being on the wrong side of those trades.

But what about Milton? Milton Friedman was a very smart man and a very great economist remarkable for his clarity of thought. Naturally "the Friedman argument" has always given us pause. Who are we to disagree with Milton Friedman? What were the odds that we were right and he was wrong?

Very poor, as it turns out. Because he never said it, at least not in the way the story is usually told. We first caught on to this possibility when we noticed that the Friedman argument, while often referred to, is rarely cited: it doesn't show up in the footnotes. It has become part of general economic lore. We have seen at least one paper by a highly respected professor of finance who simply referred to "the Friedman argument" as part of the "oral tradition."

It isn't. The Friedman argument, we eventually discovered, comes out of a very real paper, published in 1953 as part of a collection called "Essays in Positive Economics," but based on previous work Friedman had done as a consultant for the U.S. government's effort to rebuild the economies of Europe after WWII. The paper makes the classic Friedman argument very clearly: Smart money in the market is constantly arbitraging away price mistakes made by dumb money; over time this process deprives dumb investors of their capital and influence in the market, leaving the market dominated by smart money investors who arbitrage away all mispricings at great speed.

So what's the problem? Simple. Friedman was not talking about equity markets, which have been the overwhelming focus of the argument and the empirical research on efficiency. He was not even talking about bond markets, which we would argue (contrary to conventional wisdom) are more efficient than equity markets. So was he writing about commodity markets? Nope, not even commodity markets.

He was writing about currency markets. And he was writing about them in an article that has little to say about market efficiency in general. The paper, titled "The Case for Flexible Exchange Rates" is an argument for floating rather than fixed currencies; the Friedman argument simply comes into it as a way of illustrating how the mechanism would work.

Currency markets are a very special case of all financial markets, so special that one can hardly call them efficient or inefficient. If the EMH means anything, it means that markets get prices right, or pretty right. Right has only one possible coherent meaning: The price of a stock is right to the extent it accurately reflects the value of the assets on which that stock represents a claim. The price of a stock is in effect a price sticker appended to a definable pile of assets. The value of the assets, in turn, is best defined as the present value of all future cash flows from those assets. We cannot know for sure whether a price was right until the cash flows are delivered. Still, in many cases we can develop rough estimates, grounded in rough valuation of particular assets. We may not be able to get prices very right, but at least we know what we are trying to price.

This is not a coherent description of floating currency prices. True, a floating currency is in some sense backed by all the assets of the issuing nation. But there can be no pretense to even roughly measuring from those assets to currency prices, nor any pretense that currency prices remotely represent such a measurement. Because currency prices in such a system cannot be coherently referred to any pile of assets, they can hardly be said to refer to anything but themselves and to other currency prices. There is no possible realistic, even approximate test for the rightness of currency prices, and no one really believes in such a test. Yes, one can sometimes coherently relate a move in the price of the dollar or the euro to some particularly dramatic event, but no one even pretends to know how to do so with any show of accuracy.

What a lot of words we are using to make a simple point. Let's sum it up in a sentence: If all the advocates of market efficiency can claim is that equity markets are as efficient as currency markets, they can have those markets on a silver platter and good riddance to them.

CHAPTER NINE

Zoom, Zoom, Zoom

A s attentive readers may recall from chapter two, in Andy's December 2006 letter to our clients we poked fun at an amazing document issued by the International Monetary Fund claiming that there was no need to worry that structured finance could destabilize the credit markets. Quite the contrary, according to the IMF, the news was all good. According to the IMF we were simply seeing the triumph of free markets in credit over the crusty old club of bankers. The result, argued the IMF, was a more liquid and transparent market, with a more diverse base of investors. These new investors included large, traditionally conservative institutional sources not previously willing to invest in the low-rated mortgages and other credit instruments that made up the ultimate asset base in most structured deals. They were suddenly willing to do so because they had been persuaded that the tranched "structure" of the deals fully determined their risk. No need for these novice investors to understand the details of the underlying credits by applying traditional credit analysis. The important thing, argued the IMF, was that relatively large and public markets were replacing relatively small and private ones.

In the IMF's ideology, which is also the ideology of modern

portfolio theory, replacing private markets with public markets must always and everywhere be a good thing. Public markets are more efficient than private markets because they improve "price discovery" (you can see prices right up on your computer screen!) and facilitate the all but instantaneous transmission of "price signals" to buyers and sellers, producers and consumers. These signals, reflecting the moment-to-moment views of thousands or millions of investors, are believed to provide much more rapid and reliable information about changes in asset value than a traditional credit analyst could ever aspire to, laboring away alone with his green eyeshades, his calculator, and his financial reports. As relatively more public markets in credit replaced relatively more private markets, market players such as banks would benefit, the IMF argued, from "better and earlier information about credit quality" provided by market prices. Paradoxically those fast-reacting markets might even adjust to new information not only more quickly but more calmly than private markets. "The increased transparency of credit pricing and credit quality that these markets provide may reduce the volatility of credit cycles."[39]

The efficient market hypothesis, which says that, on average, modern financial markets get prices right, is a fundamental axiom of modern investment theory. But underlying both the IMF's argument and the EMH itself is an even deeper assumption: The larger, more liquid and frictionless and fast-paced a market, and the greater its capacity for disseminating all price information to all participants at the greatest speed, and the more universally it encompasses within a single bidding system all interested buyers and sellers—in other words, the more any market looks like modern securities markets in all their electronic and insubstantial glory—the more likely that market is to be efficient, to get prices right, to approach the theoretically perfect market of classical theory, the market of perfect competition, perfect pricing, and thus zero profit.

This is an axiomatic, virtually unchallengeable position in our era. Even critics of the EMH, who for decades now have been piling up evidence of inefficiencies and mispricings in securities markets, rarely challenge this core assumption that financial markets are as good as it gets. Most of these critics happily concede that modern securities markets, and especially equity markets with all their zoom, zoom, zooming liquidity and fanatic obeisance to the law of one price for all buyers, are, however imperfect, the best real-world markets we have. Other markets, imply most critics of the EMH, and sometimes more than imply, are even worse.

But are securities markets the best we have? Could it be that modern financial markets, far from being the best of all possible markets, are closer to being the worst? Not the worst in every respect, of course. What modern capital markets do very well is raise large amounts of capital from a broad base of investors who are persuaded to give their money to perfect strangers with precious little idea of what these fortunate recipients are going to do with it. In order to keep the money coming in under such admittedly odd circumstances, liquidity and the universal, instantaneous "price discovery" that financial markets offer with a glance at a computer screen are essential. The public investor, knowing so little about what he is buying, must be able to tell himself he can get that money back (or what's left of it) pretty much whenever he likes. So he demands liquidity. For the same reason he insists on knowing at any given moment if not the true value of his investment, at least the price he could sell it for. Liquidity and instantaneous price discovery function as psychological crutches investors demand to justify putting their money into what, for most of them, very nearly approaches a black box.

Such "screen-based price discovery" has become crucial to the very notion of public investment. This response to the almost pathetic need of public investors for constant assurance that they could cash out for some definite price is widely held to be one of the proofs that public markets are efficient. Why is that? How does the fact of large crowds of buyers and sellers trading at a frantic pace in front of a handy screen assure that the resulting prices make sense or even "fully reflect all available information"?

Yes, screen-based price discovery does demonstrate that public financial markets adhere unusually closely to the "law of one price." This law holds that in an efficient market identical goods available with identical transaction costs should have the same price. Certainly a market that flagrantly flouted this law would be a defective one. Uninformed, amateur customers would be much more reluctant to buy stocks if different brokers commonly sold, say, IBM, for substantially different prices at the same moment.

Undoubtedly it is a good thing, in itself, that public investors in the stock market (and heavily traded bond and derivatives markets) can readily verify that everyone is paying the same price. And certainly it is a good thing, in itself, that the participation of a large number of buyers and sellers usually means that the public investor can enter and exit investments quickly. But neither of these heartening truths alters the fact that extreme liquidity and screen-based price discovery both look like markers for a market dominated by mobs.

How do public financial markets compare to other economic markets, much less fanatically focused on either liquidity or perfect price discovery?

Consider the supermarket. Supermarket shoppers do not have the advantage of gathering all buyers and sellers into a single bidding system. There are no screens at our local supermarket telling us the price of milk across town or across the country. Yet, supermarket shoppers do a *reasonably* good job of enforcing the law of one price. Some supermarkets do charge more for a tomato or a steak or even a quart of milk than others, even in the same city.

But in most cases the difference is readily accounted for by quality, location, level of service, store branding, whether an item is being used as a loss leader, and similar factors. Of course no one would argue supermarket price discovery is *as* good as it is in financial markets. Yet the remarkable thing is not how badly the retail food market adheres to the law of one price, but how well, considering its inherent limitations.

How it does this we will address in a moment. Meanwhile, equally remarkable, surely, is how confident supermarket shoppers appear to be about prices, even without screen-based price discovery for tomatoes or potatoes. Here is what we mean.

Whatever else investors in public securities want to know, the one thing they insist on, as a group, is to know what everybody else is paying at a given moment. This is so obvious that it seems odd even to remark on it. But buyers and sellers in other markets are not nearly so paranoid. They know quite well that in most markets, like supermarkets, the law of one price is not perfectly adhered to. In a very large number of cases the question cannot even be meaningfully asked, since comparing prices in different circumstances swiftly becomes an impossibly complex many-body problem. Yet buyers and sellers in most markets are not unduly disturbed. Why not? Why are they price confident without a big screen to reassure them? Why are public investors price paranoid even with a big screen backing them up? What is it that supermarket shoppers, or for that matter heavy equipment shoppers, or building trades buyers, or fashion buyers, and all the rest know that public investors don't?

Adam Smith made a distinction (that we tend to find old fashioned today) between "use value" and "exchange value," between the utility of a thing and the price it can be sold for at a given time and place. In our day we tend to avoid notions of "objective" or "use" value, or any sort of value other than the completely relative "exchange value." We make value and price synonyms. But we do this precisely in obedience to the modern theory, precisely as a result of accepting that securities markets are the paradigm of markets generally. As soon as we pinch ourselves and step outside the dream world of securities markets we have no trouble at all distinguishing "use value" from "exchange value."

The shopper who chooses between a tomato and a cucumber, a steak and a roaster knows quite well the use value of these items to her family. That knowledge provides a crucial discipline on her willingness to pay the asking price. Supermarkets include good shoppers and poor shoppers, informed shoppers and ignorant shoppers. Still, in supermarkets and most well-functioning markets of our experience the purchasers' reasonably well-grounded judgment about the use value of an item is one strong discipline on price.

Almost the only markets known to us in which this is not true are those supposed to incarnate most perfectly the paradigmatic virtues of markets generally: public securities markets and especially stock markets. In these markets, price is not well disciplined by utility for the simple reason that it is all but impossible to estimate that utility with confidence.

The use value of a stock, the value of owning it over the course of its life, is well known in theory: It is the present value of all future cash flows. It is not impossible to make a reasonable guess at that value; investors do this all the time. But it is impossible to believe that one's own estimate is likely to be right except within a very large margin of error, or to deny that even an investor who is generally good at making such estimates will frequently be very wrong. Certainly we can never be as confident of the value for us of a stock two years from now as we are of the value for us of a chicken two hours from now, or generally speaking the value of a piece of farming or manufacturing equipment over its reasonable life.

Oddly, the reason for this is that the use value of a chicken or a tractor or a sewing machine is subjective. We know it for our own case because we are the prospective users.

I do not own a farm, so a tractor is of no use value to me. The only way I could get value from a tractor would be by selling it, i.e., by getting what Smith called its exchange value. I am not well positioned to do this because I don't live in a farming community or know anyone who wants a tractor. Because I am not a farmer, know nothing about tractors, and can't readily go about buying and selling them, if for some reason I wished to invest in tractors I might be better off buying publicly traded shares in a tractor company. But what makes owning shares in a tractor company the better choice for me? Only my ignorance and the fact that I am not part of the real tractor market. The greater liquidity of a public market might partly compensate me for being clueless and unconnected with regard to actual tractors. But if I were a farmer, I would know from my own experience how much money the tractor typically makes for me in a year.[40] I would be able to evaluate any offer for my tractor against my own use value. Even in a farming community, the farm equipment market would not have a fraction of the liquidity of the stock market and would lack screen-based price discovery. But compensating for those weaknesses, the players in that market could always judge prices against a reasonably ascertainable use value.

In other words, different markets make different trade-offs between liquidity and price discovery on the one hand and confidence about value on the other. The grocery shopper purchases her groceries even though they utterly lack liquidity. She must base her purchase on the convergence of price and use value because use is her only option. The chances that the purchaser of a tomato at retail will be able subsequently to resell the tomato to "a greater fool" should she begin to doubt its value are not good.

She must make a firm judgment of value at the time of purchase; there is no going back. In other words, at the very moment the shopper buys a tomato because of its use value, its exchange value falls to near zero. This very lack of a secondary market speaks to the quality of pricing in the primary market. No investors would buy shares in a public company under such restrictions because no buyer of public shares is as confident as the buyer of a chicken in a supermarket. Even buy-and-hold investors would not buy if they could not sell. Public equity investors demand liquidity in large part because they are unsure about value.

The principle that demand for liquidity reflects skepticism about the convergence of price and value becomes particularly evident when we compare one public financial market to another. Compared to stock markets, bond markets are far less liquid and have higher transaction costs. Many bonds of lesser-known companies still trade less than once a day. Even today for many corporate bonds there is really no such thing as a published price and therefore no screen-based price discovery. They are traded by phone or e-mail. Nor does the bond market faultlessly obey the law of one price. The relatively few private investors who buy bonds of lesser-known public companies are routinely overcharged compared to well-connected professional traders and institutional buyers.

And yet no one doubts that in most cases bond prices are generally more likely to reflect the use value (the future cash flow) of the bond than stock prices are to reflect the use value of the stock. For as with a tomato or a chicken or a tractor, in most cases we pretty well know what's "in" a bond. Absent default, we know how much cash flow is left through maturity just as we know how many people can be fed by a roaster. Equity investors, by comparison, haven't a clue what's "in" their share of stock, and so they are ferocious in their demand for liquidity and price discovery. It is not liquidity or perfect price discovery that ensures good pricing but knowledge of value. It is when we lack this knowledge that we demand liquidity and price discovery as poor substitutes.

Of course we have rather coyly been avoiding the most crucial discipline of all in equilibrating value to price: cost. In a market at equilibrium—the theoretic market of perfect competition, complete knowledge, and zero "true profit"—the price at which an item sells is limited by the fully accounted cost of production including all management and transaction costs. This is true for the simple reason that if a competitor could readily and profitably undersell, he would.[41] In the real world, markets are rarely, if ever, so efficient. Nevertheless, our buyer of a tomato or a tractor can be roughly confident that the price he pays is roughly disciplined by some version of the cost.

But what is the cost of producing a share of General Motors? The question is all but meaningless. There is no reason whatsoever to believe that public markets routinely equilibrate the price of a share of GM to the cost of creating either another share or a genuine rival car company. As for verifying the cost for oneself, the value school of investing does use the notion of "replacement cost" to detect stocks that are grossly under- or overpriced. But no sensible outside investor claims any great accuracy for this process, which is why value investors insist on deeply discounted prices that incorporate a very large margin of error. Federal insider trading laws very specifically deny the typical outside investor the information needed to do a more precise job estimating either replacement value or the best use to which a firm's assets could be redeployed.

In our time the quality we associate above all with well-functioning markets is speed: the ever-increasing speed with which information about supply and demand circulates, with which new products are brought to market, with which prices are adjusted, with which buyers and sellers, producers and consumers adjust to new information. We are accustomed to think of markets as agents of change and even of revolution. But this accelerating pace of change does not actually support the classic role of markets, which is to move (asymptotically) toward equilibrium. On the contrary, in today's rapid pace of new product development we are witnessing the other great force in a successful economy, the power of entrepreneurs, multiplied by modern technology and communications, to upset equilibrium by innovating. By innovating they create the one thing that is not supposed to exist in a market at equilibrium: a genuine profit—a surplus of income after all costs are subtracted from the selling price. The whole point of being an entrepreneur is to knock markets silly, to steal a march on costs without giving in on prices, or to boost the prices you can charge by creating more use value for the same cost at which your competitors are making last year's model.

Perhaps because communications and computer technology appear to have made the introduction of new products so efficient, cycling with amazing speed through innovation and counter-innovation, to and from equilibrium, we have come to associate market efficiency with the speed with which information is circulated, exploited, and discounted. This naturally encourages the assumption that our most frantic markets, financial markets, which seem to consist almost entirely of new information being disseminated at light speed and discounted all but instantaneously, must be the most efficient of all.

Smith and the other classical theorists saw it differently. Far from being agents of change, in *The Wealth of Nations* markets appear more like forces of tradition. For Smith, efficient markets—markets that correctly equilibrate market and "natural" prices (i.e., costs)—are more like tracks gouged deep by wagon wheels that have run over the same path in the same direction carrying the same heavy loads year in and year out. The first instinct of all participants in a well-settled market is to do this year exactly what they did last year, do this September what they did last September, this Tuesday what they did last Tuesday. Try to break out of the rut and in most cases the market with all its accumulated wisdom will steer you back.

This really is where the invisible hand comes from. Smith explains that certain markets, especially commodity markets, are less good than others, such as markets for certain manufactured goods. Less good in the sense that they are less good at equating market prices with "natural" prices (costs), exchange value with use value. As an example he contrasts the volatility of corn markets in his day with the relative calm of markets for manufactured cloth.

Why was the corn market relatively volatile and the cloth market relatively stable? The market for cloth on both the demand and supply side was a relatively settled thing according to Smith. One might even say that it was institutionalized. Over the years, in the cycle of trial and error, profit and loss, bankruptcy and solvency, a certain capacity for producing cloth had been established that roughly equaled the demand for cloth at roughly the price for which it could be manufactured in that time and place. Because it is not so easy to dramatically increase capacity (for this involves raising capital, building factories, luring workers from other industries and training them, and the like) or for that matter even to dramatically reduce it (given existing commitments of capital and the need to maintain cash flow) and given that population and personal income and thus "effectual demand" do not change so rapidly either, cloth prices remained relatively stable.[42] But none of this was true for corn, for the simple reason that the exact same inputs could produce dramatically different outputs year to year, depending on factors such as weather that were both beyond the farmers' control and insensitive to demand.

All this is clear enough. But let's try for a moment to put it in terms that Smith could not have used, but which have become quite important to us. The modern economy is often called the information economy and sometimes the knowledge economy, as if those two terms were identical. But there is an important sense in which they are very different, almost opposites.

Claude Shannon, the father of information theory, taught us that "information" is that part of a communication that comes as a surprise. In the New York City subways we used to see an ad for a shorthand course saying: "F u cn rd ths msg u cn gt a gd jb." In Shannon's terms, these letters and the spaces between them constitute all the information in the message. If we were to write out the sentence in proper English—"If you can read this message you can get a good job"—Shannon would say that the additional letters did not constitute information for the simple reason that they are not necessary to understand the message. All we need to understand the message is the "coded" version. Another way of putting it is that given the coded form of the message, the full, proper English version is perfectly predictable: it would not come as a surprise.

Remember the old story about the gulag prisoners who have been confined together so long that they no longer tell each other the same old jokes? They save time by shouting out only the joke's number. For information theory, only the number is information. The joke itself, stored in both the mind of the teller and the hearer, is not. The best part of the story, in terms of information theory, is that the prisoners still laugh even at just hearing the number. Humor is surprise they say; for Shannon so is information.

If the content of the prisoners' jokes, or the unnecessary letters in the sentence, are not information, what are they? Surely one good name for that pre-existing content is "knowledge."

Knowledge is what is built into the receiving system; the reader of our coded message automatically (even unconsciously) supplies the missing letters because he has knowledge of English.

The difference between Smith's corn and cloth markets is that although both contain some knowledge and some information, the corn market is dominated by information, that is, by surprise, and the cloth market is dominated by knowledge. The shifting winds of information (speculation about weather, predictions about weather, and, when it finally comes, the weather itself) blow the price of corn hither and yon, even now, but especially in Smith's day. This flood of information (including speculation or false information) overwhelms the available knowledge, such as how many acres have been planted, etc. Modern agribusiness, to some extent, has brought stability to commodity prices by replacing information—surprise—with knowledge. It uses knowledge tools such as irrigation (we know water will be supplied), storage (we know there is existing supply to dampen volatility), and futures markets (we insure future prices, turning speculation into certainty) to reduce uncertainty about prices. Imagine how stable corn prices would be if so much corn were stored that the annual harvest were almost irrelevant to total supply. The existing knowledge represented by the corn in storage would dominate the new information about this year's crop and much of the price volatility would vanish.

By comparison to the volatility of corn markets in Smith's day, the cloth market was much more deeply grounded in well-processed, even institutionalized knowledge, so that new information affected it much less.

But where is this knowledge that underpins the cloth market? Who will tell it to us? No one, really. Most of the knowledge on which societies are built becomes reified into the customs, laws, traditions, institutions (including commercial firms), even the physical infrastructure of the society. Much of the knowledge that made up Smith's cloth market was not even consciously apparent to the participants. It had been reified into the factories that had been built, the capital committed, the workers recruited and trained, the wholesalers, the shippers, the retailers, all accommodated over time to the roughly stable effective demand for cloth, the cost of capital and labor, and all the other considerations that both determine costs and keep prices roughly equilibrated to those costs. There was dynamism in the market, certainly. Innovation in the midst of an industrial revolution would cut costs and increase demand. Still all this reified knowledge provided a stability that would have been unknown if the production of cloth had been as dependent on the weather as the production of corn.

Such a stable market, producing prices with a strong tendency to equilibrium, can, like nature itself, seem a bit magical, precisely because the knowledge that governs it is embedded rather than articulated. It is no wonder Smith's most famous metaphor was a magical one. But the hand is invisible precisely because the market itself is so tangible.

This is why the market is often compared to a calculating machine—though probably the metaphor worked better when calculating machines were elaborate mechanical devices. The mechanical guts of the calculating machine reify a great deal of knowledge and expertise. By comparison, the information we enter for any given problem is tiny. But if we overload the calculator with information, say by giving it a ten-place calculation when it can do only nine, it will malfunction.

A sudden infusion of new information—including, of course, false or unreliable information because information is simply surprise—if powerful enough can overwhelm any market, no matter how deep its knowledge base, no matter how good a job it ordinarily does equilibrating price, value, and cost. It is reasonable to call markets better or worse depending on how much information, how much surprise they can absorb before convulsing in dramatic disequilibrium, causing market players to lose faith in prices. Good markets are markets sufficiently ballasted with knowledge to resist panic.

This condition of knowledge being overwhelmed by information is almost the constant state of equity markets. Public securities markets, and especially equity and derivative markets, are bad markets because their knowledge base is thin (at least compared to the sum of what could be known about the underlying companies if shareholders were allowed to know it, or inclined to learn it). They are easily overwhelmed by information, overreacting to it even when it is reliable and relevant. Even worse, precisely because their knowledge base is so thin, financial markets take seriously a huge amount of information of very dubious value: specifically their own prices. Lacking a more substantial basis on which to make decisions, financial markets set prices to an astonishing extent by watching—prices! This is precisely what mutual fund investors do by switching their capital to funds that have had a good run. They switch to funds whose shares have run up in price. The old joke says making a fortune in the market is simple: buy low and sell high. But most of the time investors do just the opposite. Chasing rising prices they buy high and sell low.

When the efficient market theorists had just begun their conquest of academia in the 1960s, they appeared to have demonstrated that equity markets were efficient at least in the minimal sense that future price movements could not be well predicted on the basis of previous price movements alone, i.e., technical trading doesn't work, or not very well. So sure were they of this proposition that they actually named it the "weak" form of the EMH, to denote a claim so obvious it was no big deal. They admitted it was harder to prove that fundamental analysts could not beat the market. But technical traders make money? Chartists, for heaven's sake! No way! U.S. financial markets could not possibly be such pathetic failures as to permit those charlatans to make money.

Now, of course, we know it does happen. Fama himself conceded the point long ago. We ourselves use technical factors and find them routinely useful and predictive. So do lots of people. And even though lots of people know they work and therefore use them, they still work. There are few more well-documented phenomena in equity markets.

Our point is not just that the EMH guys were wrong. On the contrary, the important thing about technical factors working is what that says about public securities markets, and on this point the EMH guys were right. A market in which traders can predict future price moves solely on the basis of past price moves *is* pathetic. Traders can do this only because public financial markets are price-obsessed and price-paranoid. Financial markets are awash in price information (how many times a second does some price on some board somewhere change?) and relatively devoid of knowledge about value and cost to compare it to. Traders are desperate to know what everyone else is paying precisely because there is so little information about what anyone *should* be paying. Public securities markets have so little information aside from prices, and such a small knowledge base, that they have little to think about besides relative prices. Of course they chase their own tails.

When we were in college together we had a Russian friend whose family had gotten out of the old Soviet Union. He told us once that even though everyone knew that the official state newspaper, *Pravda*, was full of lies, everyone read it anyway. "What else could we do?" he explained to us. "There was nothing else. Lies were the only information we had. And besides, we used to tell ourselves, some of it must be true, even by accident."

What percentage of price moves in stock markets are meaningless reactions to meaningless noise? Ninety? Ninety-five? Ninety-nine? But what else do public markets have? Where is their base of reified knowledge? What is to stand against the winds of meaningless change? In the perfect market of classical dreams, equilibrium is achieved through perfect competition because everybody knows everything. In public equity markets, everybody knows nothing, which is not quite the same thing.

People do make money investing in public securities markets. Most of them do this, however, either by accommodating themselves to the inefficiency of those markets or by actually exploiting that inefficiency. The vast majority of stock market investors do roughly what modern portfolio theory tells them to. They diversify broadly, more or less buying the market as a whole, so as to get the average return, degraded by the losers as well as lofted by the winners. The advocates of the modern portfolio theory recommend this approach on the grounds that the market knows too much to be beaten. But surely most investors follow this advice simply because they know they know too little to do anything else. Diversification is always and everywhere a confession of ignorance.

The well-documented successes of value investors who successfully pick underpriced stocks refute the notion that financial markets get prices right. But it is actually the limitations of these value strategies that testify more powerfully to the defects of public markets. Given the limits of publicly available information, estimates of securities value require large margins of error. Thus precisely because of the knowledge deficit in public markets, the value investor can invest only when the gap between price and value is almost too big to be missed.

There is really only one other way to make above-average returns in public markets. That is to do what true hedge funds do: arbitrage disagreements about value implied in the divergent prices of different securities pegged to the same or similar assets while remaining agnostic about the true value of the underlying assets themselves. In other words: buy Exxon and sell Mobil if their prices imply different values for the same oil. Such trades absolutely depend on the market getting at least one price wrong for at least long enough to put on the trade.

This practice of making money from mistaken prices is a huge business in securities markets. But it is almost unknown in most other economic markets. Even such relatively pure "merchant" activities as buying goods in one (e.g., wholesale) market and selling them for somewhat more in another (e.g., retail) are not, in the real economy, premised on either the original wholesale seller or the final retail buyer making a "mistake" about value. The merchant is paid for one of two things. The first and most common is simply the work entailed in moving the goods between markets. If this is all he does, he has earned an honest living based on the going price of his labor and capital, not on the folly of his suppliers or his customers.

Beyond this ordinary workmanlike effort, the true entrepreneur may make a true profit not by merely *observing* (as the value investor does) a gap between value and price but by *creating* such a gap. He effectively transforms the perfectly reasonable purchase price of some factor of production into a bargain by getting more value out of it than is customary. He turns rocks into pet rocks or sand into silicon chips.

In the real economy, people make money in the ordinary case by working harder, and in the extraordinary case by thinking harder. In Peter Drucker's terms, the manager earns his living by doing things right and the entrepreneur by doing the right things. As a general rule enterprises in the real economy are not premised on the assumption that competitors, suppliers, or customers will simply make a mistake and give up money by accident. That may happen, but a business that planned on it would have a difficult time.

Economic markets reward added value, which is why no true economic market is a zero-sum game. Securities markets and especially stock markets are widely assumed to be zero-sum games. Both supporters of the efficient market hypothesis and most of its critics are united on this point: most transactions on public securities markets create a loser and a winner. Most of the pulsing activity and seething energy of modern securities markets is driven by the assumption that in most trades someone is making a mistake about price. The EMH guys merely claim that in the end the market is right.

One way of thinking about why stock markets seem like zero-sum games is to think about the problematic ownership shareholders have. Shareholders' odd sort of ownership is the root of what economists have long called the "public company problem." The public company problem may be summed up as the difficulty shareholders have collecting on their claims to the income and assets of companies they supposedly own. How can these alleged owners be sure they will get paid?

The shareholder has little power to preserve corporate assets, direct their use, or even to get a clear account of them. Generally speaking the law prevents him from knowing any more about this supposed property of his than any stranger passing on the street. The managers he supposedly employs know far more than he does and they aren't telling. And mounds and mounds of research as well as common sense say the interests of managers and shareholders align sporadically at best.

The most drastic resolution of this conflict is to eliminate most of the shareholders altogether by taking public companies private, as in the "leveraged buyout" or LBO boom of the 1980s. Turn public equity into private equity. These restructurings convey large equity stakes to management, which will be worth little if the company fails, and then replace most of the remaining equity with debt, shareholders with bondholders. Bondholders' claims are far more definite and enforceable than those of the forlorn public shareholder.

The advocates of private equity claim the new capital structure will do a better job of capturing existing value for investors. But that is not all they assert. They claim the new manager-owners will also *create* new value. The private owners, they say, will do better not only for themselves but also for the enterprise. Public ownership is bad not only for shareholders but also for the things shareholders own. Strong ownership is good not only for owners but for their assets.

The record of the leveraged buyout boom of the 1980s strongly supports these claims. At the time it was frequently charged that LBOs did not create value but simply shifted it from stockholders or stakeholders to greedy insiders taking advantage of their unique knowledge of the company's true hidden value. The buyout team's gain was believed to be everyone else's loss: a zero-sum game. The subsequent academic research effectively demolished this claim.

The original shareholders were certainly not bilked: the academic research on the subject says that shareholders bought out in an LBO typically got 50 percent more for their stock than its open-market value before the takeover was announced. But even after paying 50 percent more to acquire the company, on average, LBOs in the mid to late 1980s were dramatically successful, producing powerful profits for the new investors. A whole new class of high yield bondholders arose, earning equity-like returns with only a fraction of the uncertainty of most equity investments. Following a leveraged buyout, operating cash flows tended to increase dramatically, supporting the hefty profits earned by the new equity holders and the attractive payouts to bondholders. Even toward the end of the LBO boom, when many LBOs ended badly for investors because they paid too much to get the deal done, the new structures still, on average, produced large increases in operating cash flow.[43]

Thus every investor class, including the departing investors, made out well. And what about other stakeholders or the enterprise itself? At the time critics charged that the surge in operating income common to LBOs was driven by short-term economies bad for the business in the long run: massive layoffs; underfunding of maintenance as well as research and development; dragging out payables to hype short-term cash flow. Subsequent research, however, showed that most successful LBOs were not followed by significant layoffs. R&D and maintenance funding did not decline, though new capital expenditures did. Post buy-out firms did economize on working capital but not by dragging out payables. The new management compressed operating cycles and inventory holding periods. In other words, the companies made more money because they were better managed.[44]

In theory, public ownership disciplines management by using market price to signal its evaluation of management decisions. But the price signals sent by public investors are usually worthless because public investors have no sound basis for comparing price and value. The great stock-option movement was driven by the idea that aligning the interests of management and shareholders by giving the managers hefty option grants would solve the public company problem. It didn't. Public companies are managed badly not because the interests of managers conflict with the interests of owners but because public companies have no owners, properly speaking. Ownership implies more than a claim on an income stream. It implies knowledge and control, both the legal right and the effective capacity to make judgments for the good of the firm.

Shareholders have neither. Managers who try to do what share-holders want them to do serve the interest of neither managers nor shareholders because the shareholders are in no position to say what should be done, even for their own benefit. In most cases managing to please shareholders means managing with the goal of raising the share price over the relatively near term, chasing those mutual fund investors, the dumb money. Managing to the share price means managing to ignorance.

LBOs succeeded because replacing weak owners with strong owners changed the future. The fact that outsider-driven buyouts did just as well as those driven by insiders suggests LBOs succeeded not because the buyout guys were good shoppers but because they became real owners. Companies, like most assets, do better with strong owners than weak owners. Shares in public companies are called "common" stock. As with common grazing land, they create a "tragedy of the commons" in which a vital asset is destructively mismanaged because it has only weak owners, none of whom are in a position to make strong and sound judgments for its protection.

Public securities markets surrender all the characteristics of strong ownership, including depth of knowledge and power to execute judgments. In exchange, public markets gain liquidity, breadth of participation, and low transaction costs. Most economic markets do just the opposite. They are dominated by informed buyers and sellers, who happily accept the high transaction costs and limited liquidity that necessarily obtain in markets with many fewer players, buying and selling more deliberately, for use rather than resale. Securities markets, in their very anxiety to establish instantaneous and universal agreement on prices, reveal the arbitrariness and volatility of those prices. Most economic markets, by contrast, put a high value on an evident relationship between price, cost, and value and presume the rough stability of all three in a rough approximation of equilibrium. Financial markets pride themselves not on an evident relationship between price, cost, and value but on knowing the price everyone else is paying.

Structured finance imposed on the mortgage market the same tradeoffs that public securities markets make. The new rules of the mortgage market transferred trillions in American assets from strong owners to weak owners. Homeowners with substantial investments in their homes were replaced with zero-money-down buyers. Well-informed local banks were replaced with investors in particularly opaque and complex securities whose price could be only remotely compared to the value of the underlying real estate. Structured finance transformed the mortgage market, once a collection of relatively slow-moving localized markets of relatively well-informed players into something much more like modern equity markets: universal, highly liquid, widely traded by minimally informed investors, with prices set by a mob following its own tail. It was a formula for panic.

What had not changed, however, was that U.S. home mortgages, along with commercial loans to businesses (which had gone through a similar restructuring), remained the foundation of the U.S. banking system and thus of the American economy and the dollar itself.

PART III
Practical Men

CHAPTER TEN

You've Got a Friend at Freddie's

Our first intimation of trouble came in 2002 when Andy attended a road show for potential investors put on by New Century Financial, which would become one of the largest junk mortgage originators in the nation. Andy left convinced the company would go broke.

New Century's pitch was that it was doing a better job identifying mortgage customers who, though shunned by conventional banks, were actually good prospects. This is a hard business for a public company. Being better at being picky may be good business, but it is a hard way to grow and gain market share quickly, which public companies are pressured to do.

New Century was building market share with awe-inspiring speed. They could be doing this, Andy judged, only by lowering standards, not improving them. So Andy asked the New Century spokesman two crucial questions.

The spokesman claimed the average loan-to-value ratio on the company's mortgages was 75 percent. In other words, on average the homeowners had equity in their homes equal to 25 percent of the current appraised value with the rest covered by their mortgages. Since traditional mortgages require only a 20 percent down payment, for a starting loan-to-value of 80 percent, an average 75 percent loan-to-value for an entire portfolio of recent mortgages could be pretty good—depending on how you get to that average. So Andy asked the New Century guy, "Are you averaging 75 because the loan-to-value of most loans in your book is between 70 and 80? Or are you averaging 75 because you have a bunch of 50s and 60s along with a bunch of 95s and 100s?"

The presenter said he did not know, but he was sure it did not matter. It was the average that counted.

That was an unnerving answer but crucial to understanding the mortgage crisis. Obviously the less equity a homeowner has the weaker his ownership and the more likely he is to default and walk away from a mortgage. Nobody who owns 95 percent of his house walks away and leaves it to the bank. People whose stake in their homes is 5 percent or 0 percent or even negative do that more often. That's clear and the New Century guy was not disputing that. But by suggesting it was the average that mattered rather than what statisticians would call the "distribution," the New Century guy was saying much more. He was claiming that defaults are a "linear function" of loan-to-value, in effect that there is no "tipping point," no break in the curve distinguishing a strong owner from a weak one. This is certainly wrong. An owner with 40 percent equity is almost as strong and unlikely to default as one with 60 percent equity. But an owner with zero down is much weaker than one with 20 percent down. The zero down owner is much more likely to walk away than the 20 percent down owner, even though the spread between 40 and 60 and zero and 20 is the same, 20 points. The weak zero down owner has passed a tipping point where he no longer controls his own fate. If his mortgage is a short-term adjustable-rate mortgage, as most low down payment mortgages were, and the market price of homes goes down, he will be unable to sell or to refinance and he will lose his home. The quicker he leaves, the better—why make more payments staving off the inevitable?

Translation: A pool of mortgages wherein half have a loan-to-value ratio of 50 and half have a loan-to-value ratio of 100 will have many, many more defaults than a pool of mortgages all of which have a loan-to-value ratio of 75. The New Century guys either did not grasp that or were pretending not to.

The New Century guy also explained that 85 percent of their mortgages were "cash-out refis," meaning that the borrower was refinancing not only to get a lower rate but to take out in cash some of the increase in the market value of his home: An owner with a $100,000 mortgage on a house currently appraised at $300,000 replaces it with a $240,000 mortgage, leaving $60,000 down or even $30,000, pocketing the difference. When Andy asked whether New Century had researched the default experience of "cash-out refis" versus mortgages to purchase, the New Century guy replied that the company had not studied the issue but was sure that default rates for both types of loans would be similar.

There probably was not much data on cash-out refis back in 2002. But studies of corporate loans show default rates do vary depending on how the proceeds of the loan are used. Not surprisingly, debt incurred to pay off insiders (e.g., debt incurred to allow the original owners to cash out) defaults more often than debt incurred for general corporate purposes. Cash-out refis look a lot like such corporate loans.

The new buyer putting down 20 percent and the old owner taking money out of his house are doing profoundly different things. One is becoming an owner, the other is weakening his ownership. One is buying in, the other is selling out. When the founder of a company decides it is time to enjoy the good life and starts selling off his interest in the firm, even a little bit at a time, investors worry and for good reason. Weakening ownership is always perilous.

By the time Andy sat listening to the man from New Century, the United States was almost a decade into a massive campaign to replace strong owners with weak owners in the housing and mortgage markets.

In 1992 the Federal Reserve Bank of Boston published a study asserting that black Americans were significantly more likely to be turned down for mortgages than white Americans with similar credit scores and incomes. The study made a huge splash in the media and convinced Congress, the Clinton administration, and the regulatory community that something needed to be done.

The solution the government came up with, however, did not focus primarily on racial discrimination. There were already rules on the books forbidding banks to act like bigots. Instead, banking regulations were altered to require, much more forcefully than in the past, that banks get more mortgages done for lower-income borrowers and neighborhoods.[45] The effect was not to enforce existing credit standards equally regardless of race but to lower standards to accommodate people with lower incomes and with less good credit, black or white.

The Boston Fed followed up its discrimination study with a manual for bankers on how to make more mortgages to low-income and minority borrowers.[46] In hindsight the manual appears as a blueprint for what became the "subprime" and "Alt-A" mortgage markets. Though the two categories are often confused, roughly speaking subprime mortgages are those issued to borrowers with problematic credit, while Alt-A loans are given to borrowers who may or may not have credit problems but choose a loan structure very different from the traditional 20 percent down,

30-year, fixed-rate mortgage. A zero down mortgage granted to a buyer with good credit could be an Alt-A loan. Basically, subprime is an evaluation of the borrower's credit, while Alt-A means that the structure of the loan is untraditional. A loan that is both subprime and nontraditional is typically classed as subprime rather than Alt-A, which can lead to confusion. We prefer the more succinct term "junk" to cover both.

The Boston Fed manual begins with a reminder to bankers that they better get with the program or face expensive punitive-damage lawsuits for failure to comply with affordable housing laws. The manual then goes on to recommend and to justify virtually every practice that defines junk mortgage lending. It recommends that banks reconsider "arbitrary" measures of creditworthiness that they had used successfully for decades. It urges them to consider nontraditional sources of income, including unemployment benefits and welfare checks. The manual recommends "credit counseling" to help transform borrowers with bad credit histories into good credit risks. There is not much evidence that even good credit counseling improves borrowers' behavior. In practice, credit counseling quickly degenerated into a mere check-off item used by originators to justify junk loans. Countrywide actually created its own over-the-phone counseling program to qualify borrowers with impaired credit for loans backed by Fannie Mae and Freddie Mac, the government's mortgage banks.[47]

The biggest barrier, however, to low-income, poor credit-risk borrowers was the traditional 20 percent down payment. And the most important recommendation in the Boston Fed's manual was that banks should come up with ways to get around the down payment problem. A small down payment is traditionally the single strongest indicator that a borrower will default. But there was no way to make more loans in poor neighborhoods without weakening this standard. Practically speaking, the regulatory imperative to get around the down payment problem launched the nontraditional mortgage market, previously tiny and dominated by the rich and self-employed. Soon investment banks like Bear Sterns were mounting campaigns to persuade investors in mortgage-backed securities that a 5 percent down payment from a low-income family represented just as great a commitment as a 20 percent down payment from the well-to-do.[48]

In 1997, just five years after the Boston Fed study, the Urban Institute published a surprising finding. The nation's commercial banks were making progress reaching low-income and minority borrowers. Lagging behind were Fannie Mae and Freddie Mac, which had been created specifically to make it easier for Americans of modest means to buy homes. They do this not by lending directly to homeowners but by buying mortgages originated by banks or mortgage specialists. The "twins" then typically repackage the loans into mortgage-backed securities that can be sold off to investors.

By buying mortgages Fannie and Freddie supply mortgage originators more cash to make more loans. But any mortgage repurchaser could do that. What makes the twins special is that they insure the mortgages they package. If those mortgages default, the twins reimburse investors for their loss. How can they afford this generosity? For many decades, until September of 2008, Fannie and Freddie were for-profit corporations. But they received substantial government subsidies including exemption from state and local taxes and lower capital requirements than regulators imposed on commercial banks. Far more important was that although the U.S. government never legally guaranteed the debt of the twins, essentially everyone believed that in a crisis the government would keep them afloat. Backed by this implicit promise the twins could borrow cheaply and make money on "the spread," the higher rates paid by homeowners on their mortgages.

Given that history, the revelation that commercial banks were doing more than Fannie and Freddie to fund low-income borrowers in once "redlined" minority neighborhoods was profoundly embarrassing for the twins. Both soon "modified their automated underwriting systems to accept loans they had previously rejected."[49] Once again the big challenge was the down payment problem. Within a few years of the Urban Institute's report "Fannie was offering a 97 percent loan-to-value mortgage. By 2001 it was offering mortgages with no down payment at all."[50]

In the inevitable, and inevitably silly, post-crash argument over whether the government or the greedy bankers should be blamed for the mess, the government's defenders often pointed out that the regulations never forced any bank, not even Fannie and Freddie, to lower specific credit standards or make low down payment loans. That is true. The government preserved deniability. It never specified means, only ends. It did not order the banks or the twins to make bad loans. It simply required them to make lots of loans to low-income borrowers in bad neighborhoods, to make more bricks with less straw. As economist Peter Wallison has pointed out, these requirements became progressively tougher. By 2007 Fannie and Freddie were required to show that 40 percent of the mortgages they backed were concentrated in underserved areas (practically speaking, the inner cities), "and 25 percent were to be loans to low-income and very low-income borrowers."[51] That requirement was flat out incompatible with the traditional 20 percent down mortgage.

In 2002 Fannie Mae's foundation arm published a report enthusing about the firm's progress on the affordable housing front. Citing Fannie's "trillion-dollar commitment" to increase its support of such mortgages, the report credits the twins with having "introduced a new generation of affordable, flexible, and targeted mortgages, thereby fundamentally altering the terms upon which mortgage credit was offered in the United States."[52]

Even making due allowance for self-promotion, the twins were enormous factors in expanding the junk mortgage market. They did this not only by providing secondary market financing but also by conferring the approval of the financial establishment on junk mortgages. No other institutions were in a place to do this more effectively. Added together, loans the twins packaged, insured, owned, or otherwise "touched" accounted for almost half the mortgage market. In combination they constituted the most powerful, more-or-less private financial institution in the world. And they were certainly the most politically well connected, with most senior-executive positions filled by former high-level officials and consultants from past presidential administrations and Congress. The twins maintained not only a vast Washington lobbying force but local "community action" offices in most congressional districts across the country. This complex of influence allowed them to reward compliant congressman, especially from inner-city districts, with financing for local development projects. In 2006 the Federal Election Commission found that in previous years Freddie Mac had illegally sponsored more than eighty fundraisers for political candidates, mostly members of the House Financial Services Committee, which oversees the twins. More than forty of the fundraisers were in behalf of the then-chairman of the committee, Republican Michael Oxley. Freddie Mac was fined $3.8 million, the largest fine ever imposed by the Federal Election Commission up to that time.[53] The twins were an archetype of crony capitalism, the grand alliance of money and political power that people mean when they say "the establishment."

Accounting scandals breaking at Freddie in 2003 and Fannie in 2004 resulted in the departure of the CEOs of both firms. The twins sought to burnish both their earnings and their image by dramatically increasing the portfolios of mortgage-backed securities held in their own investment accounts, justifying this buildup as part of their affordable housing program. The dollar amount of mortgages securitized and sold off by the twins actually peaked in 2003. But the amount securitized by other institutions and purchased by the twins for their own investment portfolio soared over the next four years. In 2003 Fannie held $1.3 trillion in mortgage-backed securities. By the first quarter of 2008 it held $2.4 trillion. Freddie increased its MBS portfolio from $750 billion to $1.4 trillion over the same period.[54] Acquired with cheap borrowed money, the mortgage portfolios were hugely profitable for several years. In 2008 they would bankrupt both firms.

As Joe Nocera of the *New York Times* has pointed out, it is hard to see how the twins stockpiling mortgage-backed securities assembled by others, as opposed to making or insuring more mortgages themselves, helped the poor. But that was certainly the twins' position. Back in 2004, Richard Syron, the new CEO of Freddie Mac, received a now-infamous memo from his chief risk officer, warning him of the "enormous" risk he was taking in expanding Freddie's mortgage-backed portfolio. After a devastating *New York Times'* exposé of Syron's mismanagement, published in August 2008, Syron responded, "If you are going to take aid to low-income families seriously, then you are going to make riskier loans."[55]

We confess to having very little interest in whether Fannie and Freddie acquired more than a trillion dollars' worth of securities based on junk mortgages[56] because their executives loved the poor, or because they didn't want to join them. Motive will always be murky. Sincere or not, the push for affordable housing had been crucial to the decision to replace the men of green eye shades and their old-fashioned credit analysis with financial "engineers" who claimed to be able to replace the old ways with statistics and insurance. The vast sums required to extend home ownership to millions of previously unqualified borrowers could not have been raised without the alchemy of structured finance turning junk mortgages into AAA mortgage bonds. As many observers have pointed out, a very large share of the mortgages and mortgage-backed securities that went south were issued not by the twins but by other mortgage companies, banks, and securitizers. But the twins "became the biggest buyers of the AAA tranches of these subprime pools in 2005–2007"[57] when most of the worst loans were made. "Without their commitment to purchase the AAA tranches of these securitizations, it is unlikely the pools could have been formed and marketed around the world."[58]

Nevertheless, the mortgage crisis was not caused by poor people. The poor don't have enough money to bring down the U.S. banking system. Rather, once the reduction of standards for the poor became a political imperative, inevitably the bankers extended the new lower standards to higher-income borrowers.

As economist Stan Liebowitz of the University of Texas has shown, when mortgages began to default at unprecedented levels in 2006, it was not subprime loans per se that were the problem. The drastic increase in defaults came almost entirely from "innovative" mortgages to both prime and subprime borrowers.

Look at chart 1 below, which shows "foreclosures started" for subprime mortgages, both traditional fixed-rate and adjustable-rate (ARM) mortgages.[59] ARMs were much more likely to also carry low down payments and other nontraditional features. Foreclosures for both categories of subprime loans rose in 2006 as housing prices began to cool. But fixed-rate foreclosures rose only modestly remaining far below the levels reached every year from 1999 through 2003, which included the tech wreck and the 9/11 recession. Foreclosures on innovative mortgages rocketed upward.

CHART 1

Fixed and Adjustable Subprime Foreclosures Started

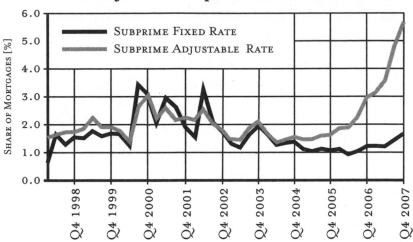

Source: Liebowitz, see note 59

Now see chart 2. Foreclosures on prime mortgages, mortgages to borrowers with good credit, show the exact same pattern. Foreclosures on traditional prime mortgages rose modestly; foreclosures on innovative mortgages went through the roof.[60]

CHART 2

Fixed and Adjustable Prime Foreclosures Started

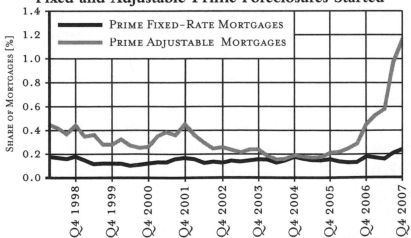

Source: Liebowitz, see note 59

Of course subprime mortgages of all sorts saw many more foreclosures than prime loans. This has always been the case. But as the charts make clear, the crisis would be driven by innovative loans that replaced strong ownership with weak ownership.

Liebowitz and others have also pointed out that the part of the mortgage market that collapsed most dramatically was the speculative market, people who bought homes to "flip" them at higher prices in a rising market. Buying to flip, once extremely rare, became a huge phenomenon, rising to 28 percent of all purchases in 2005 and slipping to 22 percent the following year. Even in 2006 the percentage of flippers began to drop only as home prices began to slip in the latter portion of that year. Though the data on "innovative" mortgage defaults do not specifically break out mortgages to speculative buyers, flippers overwhelmingly preferred innovative loans. Adjustable-rate mortgages are cheaper than fixed-rate mortgages, until they start adjusting. If you plan to sell your house in a year or two, an ARM is the way to go. Similarly, low down payments are essential to the flipper. If the flipper gets a no-recourse mortgage, which means the lender can repossess only the house and not come after the flipper for additional losses, then the flipper's down payment represents almost all his risk on the deal. Many states require that all mortgages be "no recourse."

Supporting the notion that flippers were inordinately likely to default, Liebowitz points out how rapidly defaults on innovative mortgages rose after only a slight decline in housing prices. Housing prices peaked in the second quarter of 2006. Foreclosures started to soar in the very next quarter, though home prices had still dropped only 1.4 percent nationally. A homeowner who bought to stay would likely put up a bit more fight than that. But a flipper is right to bail out as soon as it becomes clear the flip won't fly. Why continue to make payments if there will be no payoff, especially if your down payment was small and you have little to lose?

Additional evidence of speculative buying comes from the extraordinary number of people who bought homes in 2006 or later and then sent the keys back to the bank even though they could afford to make payments. According to one study, "some 18 percent of those who defaulted on a mortgage as recently as the fourth quarter of 2008 could afford their loans but simply decided to walk. Most of these defaulters . . . stay current on all of their debts and then suddenly without warning stop paying only their mortgages."[61] If your stocks go down, do you stop paying your credit card bill? No, but you may take the losses on your stocks, sell out, and move on. That's what these folks were doing, except that since they bought with little or no down payment they had nothing to sell. Their "portfolios" were "sold out" by their banks via foreclosure, just as your stockbroker may sell out your account if the value of your stocks falls to less than you borrowed to buy them.

Mortgage-backed securities shifted mortgage lending onto public securities markets. And then junk mortgages, made possible by "structured" mortgage-backed securities, made home ownership look more like investing in the stock market, or any speculative market. Whereas single-family homes had once been bought almost entirely for what Adam Smith called their "use" value, as well as an opportunity to build up ownership over the course of decades, now an astonishing proportion of homes were bought based on speculation about their short-term future market value. In the United States most investors cannot purchase common stocks with less than 50 percent cash up front, or "margin." Fifty percent is the "down payment" required for share purchases. Because banks and other investors in mortgage-backed securities believed the alchemy of structured finance relieved them from

learning about the quality of mortgages underlying their investments, speculators were able to buy homes at zero margin. "Innovative" mortgages had made the housing market potentially more
speculative than the stock market.

CHAPTER ELEVEN

If the Fat Lady Sings
and Nobody Hears Her,
Are the Canaries Still Dead?

When the mortgage market finally began to crack in early 2007 it was widely said that few people had seen it coming. So great was the supposed surprise that Andy became briefly famous for his foresight. He was even profiled by the *New York Times*.

This was nonsense. The canaries had been croaking in the coalmines for almost two years. The mortgage market was so obviously headed for trouble that by early 2006, when we started shorting mortgage-backed securities, we feared the fun would be over before we were fully invested.

We needn't have worried. Rather than the trade vanishing too quickly, we repeatedly found ourselves scratching our heads in disbelief that we could short still more mortgage securities that were obviously going to blow up. The tool most often used to short mortgage-backed secutities was a derivative called a credit default swap, or CDS. Buying a credit default swap is like buying

insurance against the possibility that a bond will default. Throughout 2006 this "insurance" on mortgage bonds stayed cheap. It was
like being allowed to buy cheap life insurance on terminal cancer
victims with a history of heart disease.

We made our first serious bets against the junk mortgage market
in late spring. As a brief review of the headlines from the *New York
Times* and the *Wall Street Journal* shows, by then the alarm bells had
already been ringing for more than a year:

WSJ July 26, 2005
Lenders Loosen Standards Despite Concerns . . .

Mortgage lenders are continuing to loosen their standards, despite growing fears that relaxed lending practices
could increase risks for borrowers and lenders in overheated
housing markets. . . . Mortgage delinquencies, meanwhile,
have remained low. . . .

WSJ November 16, 2005
Is Getting A Home Loan Becoming Too Easy?

. . . In this year's first half, New Century says, about 48
percent of its loans were less than fully documented. New
Century specializes in subprime loans, ones to people with
blemished credit records.

WSJ November 30, 2005
Consumers May Be Starting to Bend
Judging by Those Subprime Mortgages

. . . The 2005 data through September reveal that
[subprime] mortgages are faring worse than in comparable
periods in each of the three previous years. . . .

The headlines above were all from 2005. By late 2005 anyone

with even a passing interest in real estate gossip knew it was hard for anyone in America to be turned down for a mortgage and that there were a bunch of large, famous mortgage companies willing to commit blatant fraud in order to collect refinancing fees. By the spring of 2006 when feared defaults started to become real defaults, it really should have been too late to place bets against securities built up from junk mortgages. Given the onslaught of bad news, a well-functioning market should have already marked down the price of such securities, making it hard to find attractive short positions. But the market had done no such thing. It was still putting high prices on junk; good short positions were still cheap and abundant.

WSJ April 14, 2006
Foreclosures Pick Up with Midwest Hardest Hit

Nationally, the number of mortgage loans that entered some stage of foreclosure rose to 117,259 in February, up 68 percent from the same month a year earlier. . . .

Still, even with the increase in foreclosures and delinquencies, the numbers are generally not alarming to economists, as they are rising from historically low levels. . . .

WSJ May 10, 2006
Golden West Sale Might Foreshadow End to Housing Boom

. . . Before the takeover was announced, Wall Street's crack analysts were predicting that Golden West's earnings would continue to rise in a straight line, as if drawn with a ruler on a graph. . . . And then the Sandlers [legendarily successful owners of Golden West] sold out. . . . A full 29 percent of people who took out mortgages or refinanced in 2005 have no equity or negative equity in their homes. . . .

WSJ May 18, 2006

. . . *Studies Find Higher Loan Delinquencies*

Stemming from 2005's Lending Boom

. . . The Bear Stearns analysis found that, depending on the type of loan, delinquency rates were anywhere from 33 percent to 208 percent higher after the first year for most types of mortgages taken out in 2005 compared with those issued in 2004. . . .

In other words, mortgage quality had declined markedly in just one year, with 2005 loans much weaker than 2004's. In April 2006, the Mortgage Asset Research Institute crosschecked a sample of "stated income" mortgages (otherwise known as "liars' loans") against the borrowers' tax returns and found that some 60 percent had "inflated their incomes by nearly half."[62] A later Deutsche Bank report would reveal that such liars' loans made up 40 percent of subprime mortgages in 2006.[63]

So, you ask (we know you are dying to), "What did the world's newly efficient, publicly traded, up-to-the-minute mortgage markets think about all this? How did market prices "fully reflect" the information that a staggering percentage of recent mortgages had been issued by fly-by-night frauds and taken by liars who were already defaulting at record rates?" The market worshippers had been telling us for years that the new mortgage market would provide an "early warning" of distress in the underlying assets. So?

Take a look at chart 3, which should be somewhere nearby. The chart shows two indices roughly reflecting the market prices of various mortgage-backed securities issued in the first half of 2006, based on mortgages written in 2005. These indices are the basis for tradable derivatives, just like the S&P futures indices we discussed in chapter four. The indices trade more frequently and

CHART 3

ABX-HE 2006 Series 1 Closing Prices

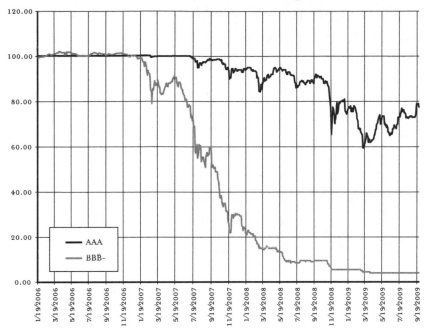

Source: Bloomberg

in more liquid markets than the individual securities themselves, so the index prices are the clearest summary we have of what mortgage-market investors believed at any moment.[64]

And in May of 2006 investors thought everything was—perfect. In the all-knowing market's view, despite the unfolding disaster out in the real world, none of these securities had lost any value. Rock solid, trading at par, every one of them. Even the BBB- tranches, much more vulnerable than the AAAs to even a modest increase in defaults, were trading at par.

This was a disaster. It was in 2005 and 2006 that the mortgage problem became big enough and bad enough to take down the nation's great banks. And it happened precisely because the new mortgage market failed to issue a warning. Would the banks have listened? They would have had no choice. The banks' balance sheets generally listed their mortgage-backed securities at market price.[65] If the market had begun to downgrade those securities earlier, in say late 2005 or even early 2006, the banks would have been forced to mark down their assets. This in turn would have reduced the volume of loans they could make. The mortgage crisis would have come earlier as homeowners found they were unable to roll their old ARMs into new. But the volume of losses sustained by the big banks would have been much less.

The years 2005 and 2006 were record ones for junk mortgages, with more money lent out at lower standards than ever before. In 2001, $2.2 trillion in new mortgages was written in the United States. Only 14 percent of those mortgages were junk of some kind: subprime, Alt-A, or home equity (wherein owners decrease their ownership by borrowing more against their homes). In 2006 almost $3 trillion in mortgages was originated. Some 47

CHART 4
Combined Loan-to-Value Ratios on 2-Year Securitized Adjustable-Rate Mortgages

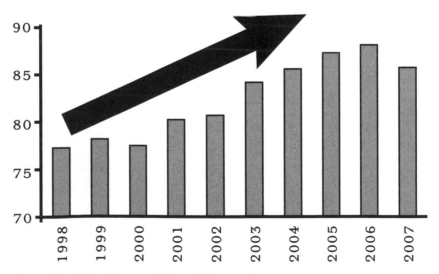

Source: The Federal Reserve Bank of Richmond

CHART 5
Subprime Mortgage Default Rates by Year Issued

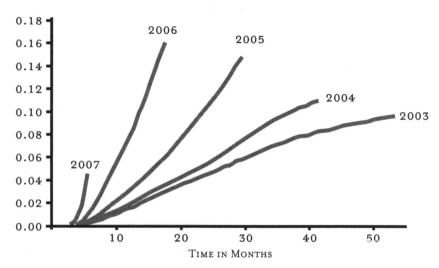

Source: The Federal Reserve Bank of Richmond

percent of those mortgages were some kind of junk, with sub-prime accounting for 20 percent alone.[66] Chart 4 shows loan-to-value ratios on securitized 2-year, adjustable-rate mortgages. The higher the ratio, the lower the down payment and the lower the loan quality. That figure rises every year from 2000 through 2006. If the graph showed only the early months of 2007, it would still be rising.

Not surprisingly, defaults on mortgages issued in 2005 and 2006, and even early 2007, far outpaced those issued in 2003 and 2004. For instance, by September 2009 the total cumulative default rate on "Option ARM" mortgages issued by private firms (i.e., not the twins) in 2005 was about 28 percent. That's a huge number. But by September 2009, the cumulative default rate on the same type of mortgages issued the next year, in 2006, was more than 46 percent, a surge of 91 percent. And the 2006 mortgages were a year younger, which means their ultimate default rate compared to 2005 loans will be even greater.[67]

Now look at chart 5. It shows the proportion of defaults on subprime mortgages issued from 2003 through 2007. Because the default rate shown is cumulative, it rises over time. But see how much more steeply the lines for 2005 and 2006 rise compared to 2003 and 2004. And the line for 2007 is nearly vertical. Not surprisingly, when the market did finally react and begin to mark down prices on mortgage-backed securities, it was those issued in 2005, 2006, and the first half of 2007 (based on loans made in late 2006) that lost most of their value. It was the mortgage-backed securities written from those periods that put the banks in danger.

Fannie and Freddie, for instance, went on a buying binge in 2005, 2006, and even into 2007. As of August 2008, almost 80 percent of the Alt-A loans owned by Freddie Mac, and nearly 60 percent of its low down payment loans, had been acquired during 2005–2007. "Between 2005 and 2007, Fannie and Freddie acquired so many junk mortgages that, as of August 2008, they held or had guaranteed more than $1 trillion in unpaid principal balance exposures on these loans."[68]

In an interview with James Lockhart, the director of the new regulatory agency created after the twins' collapse in the summer of 2008, the *Washington Post* confirmed the problem. Lockhart told the *Post* that in those years the twins "purchased and guaranteed 'many more low-documentation, low-verification, and non-standard' mortgages 'than they had in the past.' . . ."[69]

Had the market prices of mortgage-backed securities started to drop when they should have as the bad news started breaking in 2005, the twins could not have funded this huge volume of loans. The bright, new, shiny, efficient mortgage market got suckered. That made the crisis.

It should be said that the big banks themselves, along with Fannie and Freddie, were the biggest suckers. Though they sold off lots of mortgage-backed paper, they retained huge sums as well, heavily leveraged because it was AAA paper. Like the commercial bond market but more so, the mortgage security market was dominated by a relatively small number of institutions. The new market represented the worst of both worlds, public markets and private. The average institutional buyer probably knew less about the creditworthiness of the paper it was buying than the average stock or commercial bond investor knows. Yet as a specialized market dominated by maybe a few-dozen institutions for whom a collapse in prices would mean catastrophe, the mortgage-backed market included relatively few dissenters to raise an alarm. Most of the dissenters were hedge funds with only a tiny fraction of the capital of the banks and with far less access to cheap borrowed money, a.k.a. leverage. This was truly a market in which the dumb money ruled, an experts' market in which most of the experts were clueless, conflicted, or both.

WSJ July 20, 2006
Washington Mutual Net Falls 9% on Drop in Mortgage Unit Profit
. . . Profit in Washington Mutual's mortgage unit tumbled . . . to $32 million . . . from $292 million a year earlier.

WSJ July 22, 2006
. . . *Inflated Appraisals; Rosy Valuations* . . .
. . . Iowa Assistant Attorney General Patrick Madigan, who coordinates with law-enforcement officials from other states on mortgage-related issues, believes the deliberate inflation of appraisals is "widespread" among loans to subprime borrowers, or those with flawed credit histories. . . .

WSJ July 25, 2006

Do Countrywide's Loans Stack Up?

. . . the performance of the Countrywide loans generally was worse than those of WaMu, IndyMac Bancorp Inc., and Downey Financial Corp., three other big-option ARM lenders. . . .

Countrywide still has plenty of support from Wall Street . . . Paul Miller, an analyst at investment-banking firm Friedman, Billings, Ramsey & Co., in Arlington, Va., who rates the stock a "buy," says . . . "We're fine if home prices don't drop significantly."

Amazingly, Wall Street's call on Countrywide was far more optimistic than the firm's own pronouncements:

WSJ August 8, 2006

Countrywide Pulls on the Reins;

CEO Adopts Cautious Stance:

'I've Never Seen a Soft Landing'

Angelo R. Mozilo, chief executive of Countrywide Financial Corp., the U.S.'s biggest home-mortgage lender . . . has a sobering message for investors about the near-term outlook for housing and mortgages: Buckle your seat belts. . . .

So now we had Angelo Mozilo, the most famous personality in the mortgage-origination business, a man repeatedly singled out for praise for his leadership in making housing more accessible to millions of Americans, telling the world that his industry is headed for a crash. And what did markets do? Take a look back at chart 3 for August 2006 prices. Nothing. Not an eye blinked. The market was incapable of drawing a connection between rising defaults and the value of even the highest-risk mortgage-backed securities.

WSJ August 10, 2006

. . . Payments on Adjustable Loans Hit Overstretched Borrowers

. . . The portion of adjustable-rate mortgages that were at least 90 days past due has climbed 141 percent in the past year, according to a recent study by Credit Suisse that looked at loans made to borrowers with good credit. . . .

WSJ August 25, 2006

H&R Block Inc.: Delinquencies at Subprime
Unit to Result in $61.3 Million Charge

NYT September 14, 2006

Foreclosures Are Up on Some Mortgages

Foreclosures on prime adjustable-rate mortgages rose to a four-year high in the second quarter, a sign that more homeowners with good credit ratings are having trouble paying their bills. . . .

WSJ September 14, 2006

Foreclosure Figures Suggest Homeowners in for Rocky Ride

Online foreclosure-data service Reattach of Irvine, Calif., said yesterday 115,292 properties nationwide entered some stage of foreclosure last month, a rise of 24 percent from July and nearly a 53 percent increase from a year earlier. . . .

WSJ October 19, 2006

Washington Mutual's Net Falls, Squeezed by Rates, Charges

[WaMu's] home-loan operation had a net loss of $33

million, which was attributed to the "difficult" mortgage market.

Then on October 19, the *Wall Street Journal* offered us this gem:

> *Though New Data Show Rising Delinquencies,*
> *Lenders Continue to Loosen Mortgage Standards*
>   . . . In a speech to the American Bankers Association this week, Comptroller of the Currency John Dugan noted that bank regulators have seen a "significant easing" of mort-gage-lending standards this year, even though banks nor-mally tighten standards when the housing market cools.

The paradox of loosening credit standards while the housing market was softening was not really such a paradox at all. The driving force of all bubbles is the overextension of credit, at first because lenders flush with money and hungry for yields begin to fund questionable projects; next because investors become des-perate not to be left out of the new best thing; and in the end because the banks are terrified that shutting the spigot will bring the whole thing crashing down. By mid-2006 we were clearly entering the last stage.

The alternative to loosening credit standards in 2006 was watching the whole business collapse. Mortgage originators live on refis. As the New Century guy had explained to Andy years before, something like 85 percent of their business was refinancings. In order to keep that business going at the same time that housing prices were beginning to crack, mortgage originators had to loosen standards. If you put down $30,000 on a $300,000 house, taking out a $270,000 mortgage, your loan-to-value ratio is 90 percent. If the value of the house slips by just 5 percent to

285, your loan-to-value has risen to almost 95. When it is time to refinance, the mortgage company will have to either lower its standards or turn you down, undercutting its own business.

This is exactly what happens when the stock market declines, except that most stock brokers don't have such round heels. If you borrow $50 from your broker to buy a $100 stock, and the stock price then drops to $75, the entire $25 loss is yours. That means you now have only $25 equity in a $75 stock. Your broker won't like that and will ask you to put down more money. But with 85 percent of its customers in the same boat, if New Century and other mortgage brokers had insisted on more margin, their businesses would have disappeared.

If the mortgage originators had a problem, then so did the banks that funded them. The banks, for instance, funded the "warehouse" stage of the process—the time from the origination of the loans to the time they were bundled and resold as mortgage-backed securities. Typically the banks wrote short-term "puts" on the mortgages that would force the originators to repurchase the mortgages if the early stage default rate exceeded a certain trigger. As default rates mounted, the big banks faced the risk that the originators, always short for cash, would not be able to buy back their loans, now lower quality than ever. And the banks needed the originators to stay out there, refinancing bad loans, because the alternative was a general collapse of the mortgage market.

So many banks, like the originators, instead of backing away waded deeper in. In some cases the banks expanded their own lending to endangered originators. In other cases they bought them outright. Both moves seemed calculated to forestall a dangerously embarrassing collapse of fly-by-night firms that owed the banks billions. In August 2006 Morgan Stanley spent more than $700 million to buy subprime mortgage underwriter Saxon. A month later Merrill bought California home-lender First Franklin Financial for $1.3 billion. Both Morgan and Merrill claimed these acquisitions would enhance earnings. We were skeptical. WaMu had already announced earnings reversals on its mortgage unit; H&R Block had conceded its foray into home financing had been a disaster; and Countrywide, New Century, and others had already visibly commenced their crack-ups. It seems unlikely that any bank was buying mortgage originators to "enhance earnings" in August 2006.

In late 2006 one story really rang the bell for us. In November, H&R Block announced its intention to leave the mortgage business. Block's mortgage unit, enormously profitable for several years, had issued almost $30 billion in mortgages in 2006, making it the sixth largest lender. There had been lots of ominous news before. But the Block announcement was hard news about supply and demand. A major source of easy money was getting out. Mortgages would be measurably harder to get. Homes would be harder to sell. Prices would continue to fall.

About December of 2006, the bad news reached a tipping point. The *Times*, among others, headlined a new study predicting that some 20 percent of recent subprime mortgages would end in foreclosure, a figure that made a mockery of all the historically based models. Two originators filed for bankruptcy in the first days of the month.

Finally, the "early" warning system kicked in and mortgage markets began to react. In late December of 2006, the cost to insure a BBB- mortgage bundle against default had been about $400 for $10,000 worth of bonds. By the end of February 2007, the price for the same amount of insurance was tickling $2,000. The market for the lower-rated tranches of mortgage-backed securities began to vanish. The index for BBB- tranches issued in the first half of 2006, which had been selling for par or 100 in

December, lost more than 20 percent of its value by late February (see chart 3 on page 149). The AAA tranches would not begin to slide until late summer.

Over at the *New York Times*, Gretchen Morgenson began to call attention to a curious fact. All through 2006, despite "lenders going bankrupt, stocks of issuers falling, default rates on new loans well above historical averages," the government-approved and regulated ratings agencies had refused to revise their sunny outlook on mortgage-backed securities. In 2006, she pointed out, Moody's "downgraded only 277 subprime home-equity loan tranches, just 2 percent of the home-equity securities rated by the agency. . . . . Among the 2005 and 2006 issues, many of which are defaulting at high velocity, Moody's has put 62 tranches on review for possible downgrade. That is less than 1 percent of the total subprime deals rated in those years. . . ."[70]

The ratings agencies are supposed to lead the markets not follow, provide a check not an echo. But that's what they became. As long as the market continued to "rate" a mortgage-backed bond at AAA by pricing it at par, the ratings agencies went along. Just as in the stock market most "information" consists of price changes generated by the market itself, the ratings agencies recycled market prices as credit ratings. Only when the market collapsed did they revise their ratings downward.

Last to let go of the dream were the big banks themselves. New Century Financial at one point had more than $17 billion in lines of credit from the Morgans, Goldmans, and such of the world. Even after New Century announced on February 7, 2007, that it would have to restate its earnings for the previous three quarters, Goldman extended for three more months a line of credit originally set to expire on February 15. Only in the first week of March after New Century announced it was the target of a federal criminal investigation, as well as inquiries by the SEC, the NYSE, and, for all we know, the RCMP, did its Wall Street lenders finally cut off the money.

As for the regulators and the rest of the government, they were right on top of things as always. On February 27, 2007, the very same day that the lower-rated mortgage-backed indices began to collapse but almost a full week before the announcement of criminal charges against New Century, Freddie Mac, in a bold move, announced it "would tighten lending standards and stop buying certain risky kinds of home loans." (Not everyone was pleased. Mr. Kurt P. Pfotenhauer, a senior vice president with the Mortgage Bankers Association, indignantly protested that though it was true that a record 13.5 percent of subprime borrowers were in default, Freddie should try looking at the glass as half full. "Put another way," Pfotenhauer whimpered, "86.5 percent of people who have subprime ARMs are paying on time.")[71]

Not every bureaucracy responded to the crisis with Freddie's alacrity. It was not until almost a week later that the Office of the Comptroller of Currency, the Federal Reserve, the Office of Thrift Supervision, the Federal Deposit Insurance Corporation, and the National Credit Union Administration banded together to propose a new set of regulatory guidelines suggesting that "banks that make adjustable-rate mortgages to people with weak, or subprime, credit should consider the ability of the borrowers to pay back the loan. . . ."[72]

CHAPTER TWELVE

Into Great Silence

And then . . . nothing happened.

Or remarkably little, anyway. The market prices of the lower-rated tranches of mortgage-backed securities, which had lost more than 20 percent of their value by late February of 2007, actually recovered much of that loss during the spring. They did not begin to slide again until mid-May. By definition, however, the lower-rated tranches made up a small minority of all the mortgage paper out there. The prices of AAA paper, which existed in much larger volume, were still holding steady.

Ownit Mortgage Solutions Inc. filed for bankruptcy in early spring of 2007. When it collapsed it owed Merrill almost $100 million. Joining the fallen were Mortgage Lenders Network, which had been lending at an annualized pace of more than $12 billion a year in late 2006, and New Century Financial. Amazingly, as late as August 2007, Countrywide was able to raise a $2 billion loan from Bank of America to keep going. The bank eventually ended up owning the mortgage firm.

Within a few months mortgages had gone from being way too easy to get to probably too hard to get. Otherwise as late as mid-2007 neither financial markets, other than the mortgage market itself, nor the government gave much sense of shifting into crisis mode. Andy's prediction that credit markets would go into crisis as a result of a mortgage-market collapse had bought him his fifteen seconds of fame. Nevertheless, this prediction had not—yet—come true. In Andy's December 2006 client letter predicting the mortgage blow-up we had predicted that credit spreads (the gap between the rate on Treasury paper and some other security) on high yield instruments would exceed 10 percentage points (or 1,000 basis points, or bps, as the pros say). But as late as June of 2007 spreads were not only lower than when we had written the letter but were barely over 225 and near all-time lows. In other words, even companies with relatively poor credit could borrow money at a rate only 2.25 percentage points higher than the U.S. government! The high yield spread would not actually exceed 1,000 bps until 2008.

In June 2007 the system got its biggest shock yet when two large in-house Bear Stearns hedge funds specializing in mortgage debt suspended redemptions (basically investors were told they could not withdraw their money until further notice). Merrill Lynch, a creditor of the funds, responded by seizing some $800 million worth of the funds' assets. But when Merrill tried to auction off the mortgage paper it seized, it found most of it unsellable. In the third week of July, Bear announced that the two hedge funds had lost essentially all their value—the investors' money was gone.

This was a big, big deal. It made a lot of news. Most striking, though, was what remained unsaid. As the estimable Jim Grant, of *Grant's Interest Rate Observer*, pointed out at the time, the resolution of the Bear crisis did not include a sale of the impaired mortgage assets held by the fund. Grant suspected that no one really wanted to know for sure how low prices could go in a massive sell-off. Under "mark-to-market" rules, those prices would become part of the accounting standard for valuing the mortgage-backed holdings of other banks. That might create huge paper losses for the banks, crippling their ability to lend, driving home prices even further down, and, perhaps, revealing the banks as insolvent. At this point, not one major bank had taken a significant write-off for its exposure to the mortgage market.

On July 19, 2007, the Dow closed over 14,000 for the first time ever. In the mind of the all-knowing market, all was bliss.

Within weeks, the big banks began to crack.

Citibank was a fairly typical story. On October 1, 2007, the bank announced a $5.9 billion write-down of its assets (which it had "pre-announced" in August). This was about 15 percent of the $40 billion or so it would write off by spring 2008. On the same day, UBS announced a $3.4 billion hit (less than 10 percent of its eventual total). In both cases the stock market actually cheered. Both banks worked hard to create the impression that they were behaving conservatively by acknowledging a temporary downswing in market values. Citi's $5.9 billion write-down even included $2 billion in reserves against future problems. Its stock closed up 2 percent in the wake of the announcement; UBS stock gained more than 3 percent on the day.[73] Charles Prince, the CEO of Citigroup, predicted the company would "return to a normal earnings environment in the fourth quarter."[74]

Instead, on November 4, Citi announced that the fourth quarter would bring additional write-downs, ranging from $8 to $11 billion, because of deeper losses in the mortgage market. This time CEO Prince resigned. Former Treasury secretary Robert Rubin stepped in as chairman of the board.[75] The company refused to make any further predictions.

Citi's fourth-quarter write-down turned out to be neither $8 billion nor $11 billion, but $18.1 billion—$17.4 billion of it driven by further declines in the bank's mortgage-backed portfolio. New CEO Vikram Pandit announced the bank would raise

$14.5 billion in new capital.[76] In April 2008 the company would announce another $15 billion lost on mortgages.[77]

From October 2007 through April 2008, write-downs that Citi had originally estimated at $5.9 billion ballooned to almost $40 billion.

At Merrill, the first announcement came on October 5, 2007, when the firm said it expected to write off about $4.5 billion on its mortgage- and asset-backed securities. Just days later, on October 24, Merrill almost doubled that figure, officially announcing a write-down of $8 billion. "Our assessment of the potential risk and mitigation strategies were inadequate," hazarded then-CEO Stan O'Neal.[78] Standard & Poor downgraded Merrill's senior unsecured debt from AA- to A+ and called the $8 billion loss "startling."[79] It is not recorded whether the rating agency was startled again three months later when the firm announced another nearly $16 billion in mortgage write-downs.[80]

In late 2008, after writing down almost $30 billion total in mortgage- and asset-backed paper, and with more undisclosed problems on its books, Merrill would cease to exist as an independent firm, bought out by a reluctant Bank of America under pressure from the U.S. government.

Morgan Stanley was a relatively minor player in the mortgage market. Some observers had predicted it would escape undamaged. Morgan's third-quarter earnings release issued on September 19 was positively giddy, with a headline celebrating "Record Net Revenues, Net Income, and EPS for First Nine Months of FY07." The company did note "losses of approximately $940 million due to the marking-to-market of loans as well as closed and pipeline commitments." These write-downs were ascribed to "illiquidity created by current market conditions." Illiquidity is what you call it when you are still praying that plummeting market prices of stuff you paid a lot more for reflect merely a temporary market spasm.[81]

Less then two months later, Morgan "pre-announced" a $3.7 billion dollar write-down on "U.S. subprime and other mortgage-related exposures." It wasn't enough. By the time Morgan's fourth quarter and fiscal year finally ended on November 30, the loss had grown to a total of $9.4 billion for the quarter.[82]

Dozens of other banks followed the same pattern—clear sailing and happy talk all summer and then write-downs of billions of mortgage paper in the third and fourth quarters of 2007 and into mid-2008.

Had the banks been lying all spring and summer, covering up the looming catastrophe? The unnerving answer is that the banks almost certainly did not know in early June that they would be forced to announce write-downs of this size just three months later. Starting in late summer, something had changed.

What was that? Did lots of borrowers who paid up in June all choose August to default? Did hundreds of billions in mortgages that looked good in early summer turn foul by fall?

Defaults, already high, did continue to rise rapidly at least on adjustable-rate mortgages. Defaults on even prime ARMs were on their way to record levels, double the rates of 1998 and 2001, both troubled years.[83]

Default rates, however, did not directly cause the bank write-downs. The write-downs were a phenomenon of public markets. Starting in mid-summer the market price for lower-rated mortgage securities began to fall so swiftly that AAA mortgage securities finally began to be dragged down with them. The same market that all through 2006 failed to send up the "early warning signal" that the market idolaters promised had finally decided that mortgage-backed securities were "toxic." The ratings agencies, facing accusations of gross irresponsibility, had begun downgrading more mortgage paper. That forced many institutions forbidden from holding lower-grade paper to sell immediately. Soon markets reached a tipping point where no institutional fund manager with any sense of self-preservation would own this stuff, if he could get rid of it. The market had voted. The banks had no choice but to adjust their balance sheets and adjust them again and again to market prices in free fall.

To see this, look at chart 3 (which we repeat here from an earlier chapter) that charts the fate of asset-backed securities issued in the second half of 2006, which bundled mortgages from the first half of 2006, when some of the worst mortgages were written. By late summer of 2007, BBB- prices had fallen to levels that suggested that paper could be completely wiped out by defaults. (Much of it eventually was.) Remember, the lower tranches of a mortgage-backed security typically absorb all losses from default before the next higher tranche is affected. With the lower tranches

CHART 3
ABX–HE 2006 Series 1 Closing Prices

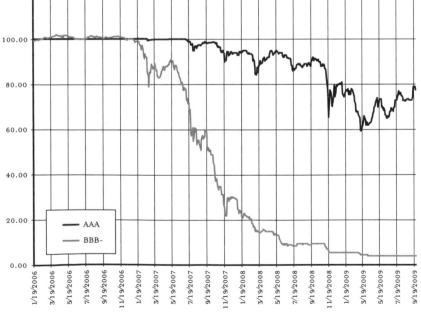

Source: Bloomberg

headed to zero, the higher-rated paper would no longer have a cushion beneath it. Suddenly AAA paper, which by definition should have a default rate close to zero, was at risk of having a default rate—higher than zero. Exactly how high no one knew, certainly not at the time.

It almost didn't matter. Institutions that buy lots of AAA paper arrange their businesses in expectation of zero defaults. For AAA investors "some" is huge compared to zero. This is especially true for banks, which operate on a small capital base and on mostly borrowed money. Under the influence of modern portfolio theory, the banks had stockpiled AAA mortgage securities believing their performance as an "asset class" was predictable. And, as the MPT prescribed, they had purchased the securities with borrowed money (e.g., from their depositors) so as to "leverage" up the risk/return parameters of their portfolios. This must have seemed like a way to "technically" increase risk/return without really increasing uncertainty. In theory a highly leveraged portfolio of predictable, low-risk securities should yield the same results as a less-leveraged portfolio of more volatile, more risky securities. But in practice, even managers who believe they believe in the MPT feel more comfortable starting with nice stable AAA securities and leveraging up than buying more speculative securities and holding leverage low. And then of course most institutional investors, and certainly the banks, are discouraged by law or policy from owning highly volatile securities like stocks and encouraged to hold supposedly stable paper like AAA bonds.

Buying AAA paper and leveraging up had looked like a way to make good money without having to do what entrepreneurs do: make judgments under uncertainty.

Now, suddenly, AAA mortgage paper looked uncertain indeed.

When AAA paper begins to look bad, its typically conservative owners tend to dump it very quickly if they can. Once doubts began to set in, AAA mortgage-backed paper first stumbled, then fell, then collapsed.

Under "mark-to-market" rules the banks had no choice but to take write-downs that reflected the collapse in the market value of mortgage-backed securities. By choosing to hold their mortgage portfolios in the form of extraordinarily complex publicly traded securities, the banks had yielded control of their balance sheets to the moods of the market. True, it was a market the big banks themselves dominated. But no cartel can support prices for long in a crisis. One hole in the dike can bring on the flood.

At this point we can almost hear our readers shouting the obvious questions: "Was the market, which had clearly been overrating mortgage paper all through 2005, 2006, and even the summer of 2007, getting it right, now? Or was it being too gloomy where it had once been too cheerful?" Specifically, you'd like to know, "If the prices of AAA mortgage-backed securities drop to, say, 35 cents on the dollar (which some did), does that mean the actual mortgages, or even the actual homes, referenced by those securities were really worth only 35 cents on the dollar? And if the houses were worth more than 35 cents on the dollar, doesn't that mean that the banks' balance sheets were 'really' better than they looked?"

Unfortunately these apparently crucial questions were essentially meaningless, certainly at the time. Meaningless first because, as noted, the banks were not prepared for their AAA paper to be marked down at all. Realized losses of just a few percentage points can be devastating to institutions leveraged twenty or thirty times over. Moreover, under the structured finance regime, as default rates rose the already opaque relationship between the value of any mortgaged property and the various securities that might have some claim on that property became staggeringly complex.

The normal, straightforward process of unwinding a failed mortgage by auctioning off the property and dividing the proceeds has shockingly little to do with what happens when an interlocking complex of structured securities begins to fail. And then there are the derivatives, the credit default swap "insurance policies" on the securities, which some of the banks also held in large quantities, raising such complicating questions as, "Do the firms that sold insurance actually have the money to pay off, now that the insured securities are failing?"

We don't want to go quite so far as to say that it was theoretically impossible to establish a relationship between Tom's, Dick's, or Harry's mortgage and any particular pile of structured paper on, say, Citigroup's balance sheet. And we know today that the damage sustained by Tom, Dick, and Harry was devastating. But it certainly was practically impossible at the time for any investor, including the major players, to say with any confidence or credibility whether market prices were "right" or what their holdings were "really" worth.

Low down payment, adjustable-rate mortgages with fishy documentation had made Tom, Dick, and Harry weak owners of their own homes. Now the investors in mortgage-backed securities, the ultimate funders and theoretic co-owners of Tom's, Dick's, and Harry's houses, were being exposed as barely owners at all. If an investor does not know even what assets he has a claim on, or have a ready way to figure how the degeneration of those assets affects the value of his claim, his ownership is nil. Trillions in assets were being revealed as orphans.

Consider the tale of Deutsche Bank's late 2007 attempt to foreclose on fourteen Ohio homes whose owners had fallen behind on their mortgage payments. Showing up in court for what they expected to be a routine process, the bank's lawyers were stunned to hear the judge ask a rather obvious question, "Could the bank demonstrate its legal title to the homes?" A mortgage conveys the title, so let's see it, demanded the judge. No go. Deutsche Bank's claim was mediated through a typically complex mortgage-backed security and all it had was a document stating the "intent to convey the rights in the mortgages." Not good enough said the judge and the bank left empty-handed, at least that day. For all we know, the bank eventually got its houses; "show me the mortgage" did not become a general defense. But that it could be done even once, even temporarily, is emblematic of how much had been staked on so little information.[84]

Where were regulators while the banks were miring their balance sheet in these complexities? Encouraging complexity every step of the way. Essentially every government of the major economic powers had encouraged the migration of mortgages to public markets. The first Basel accord, an agreement among these governments on standards for banking regulation, assertively encouraged replacing traditional mortgages with mortgage-backed securities.

Growing complexity in the banks' assets in turn demanded complexity in the accounting for those assets, and especially accounting for risk. To meet this need the banks began to develop extraordinarily complex "black box" statistical models to measure the risks they were taking. Necessarily, the inputs to these models were often the outputs of other complex models, such as the valuation models for mortgage securities criticized by Frank Fabozzi and others. (See chapter two.) These systems come in various flavors but are generally called Value-at-Risk, or VaR models. VaR models yield a number, a dollar figure representing the maximum loss a bank's investments are likely to sustain within a given time period, typically twenty-four hours or a few days. Most companies use a 99 percent probability VaR, which means that the probability of losing whatever the VaR number is—say $100 million—in, whatever the period is, say, twenty-four hours—is less than 1 percent.[85] VaR assures the bank that it is not unknowingly on the edge of the abyss.

The Basel II Accord explicitly allowed the worlds' banks to use VaR systems to measure the risks to their own balance sheets. The level of risk in turn would determine how much of its own capital a bank would be required to hold against a possible disaster. Good VaR numbers would allow the banks to use more borrowed money—leverage—and less of their own capital to support their loans and investments.

Nassim Nicholas Taleb, author of *Fooled by Randomness* and *The Black Swan*, has become famous as a critic of VaR, his chief criticism being that VaR offers a false sense of security because the BAD THING that happens 1 percent of the time can be so bad that it can destroy the firm. In other words, even if the bank is right about the chance of disaster being only 1 percent, VaR typically underestimates the consequences. Taleb's criticism is right so far as it goes, but he actually understates the problem. The real danger of VaR was the same as that of all statistical systems that become substitutes for human judgment. By encouraging bankers to surrender their judgment, VaR radically increased the possibility of disaster. By justifying the bank in holding portfolios so complex that only a black-box computer model could keep track of the resulting risks, VaR encouraged banks to multiply complexity and risk alike. The danger was not that bankers using VaR would overlook a 1 percent chance of total disaster. The danger was that by checking their judgment at the door, they boosted the probability of disaster toward 99 percent.

In Andy's monthly client letters we had editorialized at perhaps exhausting length on the dangers of VaR. Inevitably, we argued, once managers put a VaR model into place, they would manage to the model and cease to challenge its assumptions. This, we wrote, is why one never hears of any financial institution "disclos-ing persistently bad VaR numbers. Excluding outright fraud, there is only one reasonable explanation: once a [bank] adopts VaR the managers manage to it because they . . . have no choice but to keep the VaR numbers shiny for their clients as well as for their own internal risk managers." This is extremely dangerous, "for VaR is a complex formal system. The essence of all formal systems is to carve away some information so as to cast what remains into bold relief, to make choices about what is important and what is not. And the truth about all models that exceed a certain point of complexity is that things left out eventually become invisible even if they never become insignificant."

VaR models could not incorporate a model for the perfor-mance of "liars' loans" because such loans had never existed as a class before. (Liars themselves go back quite a ways.) Another thing the banks' models missed was exactly what Yale's Frank Fabozzi (see chapter two) had predicted. The "pathway" of mort-gage-backed securities prices had proved to be extremely volatile. With the bank's balance sheets based on market prices the banks could look fine one month and be headed for the abyss the next, which is more or less what happened.

The VaR models failed disastrously. Morgan Stanley's third-quarter 2007 earnings release stated that the "total aggregate aver-age trading and non-trading VaR was $91 million" for the quarter and had actually been reduced by quarter's end.[86] Two months later Morgan announced $3.7 billion in write-downs. Citibank's published VaR for the end of 2006 before it started on the path of writing $40 billion off its balance sheet was $106 million. Why? The bank excluded its mortgage-backed portfolio from its VaR calculations because the mortgage securities were too hard to value accurately.[87]

When it became clear that fluctuations in market prices were gutting the big banks, some critics clamored for the government to drop the recently tightened mark-to-market rules and allow the banks to value their books the old-fashioned way. But when the SEC tightenecd mark-to-market rules in 2006 it was simply recording the triumph of the reigning ideology of finance. Once the banks replaced old-fashioned mortgages with publicly traded securities, the SEC had no real choice. Logically the rules, dating from the 1990s, should have been tightened years earlier.

If a bank's assets are kept in any form other than cash, there must be a rule for valuing those holdings. Prior to 1938, banks valued their assets at "market," at what they could sell them for in the present moment. Because market values were so impaired by the Great Depression, these old mark-to-market rules curtailed a banks' capacities to lend or even drove them to bankruptcy. The Roosevelt administration belatedly dropped the mark-to-market rule in 1938 and adopted a "historical cost" rule. Banks would value, say, mortgages on the purchase price of the home at the time the mortgage was made. Auditors could make needed adjustments over time.

In the decades after 1938, the idolaters of public markets argued that "historical cost" was both too conservative and potentially corrupt. Historical cost accounting made the banks look poorer than they really were, meaning fewer loans would be made or mortgages written. Historical cost was, in this view, "anti-market," even anti-capitalist.

It is the efficient market theorists, however, who are hostile to real markets, even to real capitalism. Blinded by their devotion to public markets, they lose faith in markets with less visible mechanisms, less readily quantified to the standards of social science. Historical cost accounting did not remove the valuation of bank assets from the market; it linked them to the right market at the time.

The default rate on traditional 20 percent down, 30-year,

fixed-rate mortgages is largely insensitive to housing prices. A bank that holds mostly such mortgages in its portfolio, and is prepared to hold those mortgages until maturity, has little reason to adopt the "price paranoia" typical of public markets, to go rushing about checking prevailing home prices, or even default rates, to see if the collateral on those mortgages should be marked down. What the bank needs to know is simply whether the homeowners are likely to keep making their payments. In most circumstances, nearly all homeowners with traditional mortgages and good credit do just that, a record that held even through the crisis.

The relevant market for traditional mortgages consists of the competing banks and their customers negotiating mortgage terms. Historical cost accounting works just fine for that market. Of course that little clutch of people does not look much like zooming modern financial markets, the principal difference being that they are not an ill-informed mob. But now the mob had been put in charge, albeit a mob of white-shoe institutional money managers, and the market price of mortgage securities became the crucial reference point. Individual mortgages rarely experience a publicly observable "valuation event." Mortgage-backed securities have a valuation event every time some similar security trades somewhere. A bank can hardly claim the mortgage-backed securities it owns are worth $10 billion when a similar bundle just sold for $5 billion.

The critics of mark-to-market made some valid points. The rules played a huge role in transforming crisis into collapse. Nevertheless the rule reflected the deepest values and the deepest fears of the financial establishment. That entire establishment, more or less, had committed itself to the idea that public securities markets represented the best method known to mankind for valuing financial assets. The securitization of the mortgage market, they believed, would banish all the eccentricities and miscalculations, irrationalities and prejudices, human error and

geographic limitations fettering the old-fashioned lending business. Credit would be perfectly priced and portioned in one single, global, virtually frictionless market.

Well maybe not *perfectly.*

CHAPTER THIRTEEN

Strategic Ambiguity

As 2007 drew to a close, markets craved answers to three crucial questions.

What was the true financial condition of the great banks, especially their mortgage portfolios?

How did the U.S. government define its role and responsibilities in the banking system at moments of extreme crisis?

Finally, which institutions did the banking system include? Only federally insured banks? Or also investment banks like Merrill or Bear or Goldman, which are neither members of the Federal Reserve system nor insured by the FDIC? Or any financial institution that is simply "too big to fail"?

But the government wasn't talking. The government was practicing "strategic ambiguity."

"Strategic ambiguity" is the phrase commonly used to describe our policy on Taiwan. No U.S. treaty or official policy statement obliges the United States to defend Taiwan should China invade. Instead we try to discourage an invasion precisely by being unclear about how we would react to one. We employ strategic ambiguity. We even talk about strategic ambiguity and go around telling everyone we are being ambiguous on purpose.

Governments love strategic ambiguity. It is a way of increasing their power, their reach, and even their credit on the cheap. Strategic ambiguity is like "leverage" in the financial world. Even sound companies borrow money to extend their assets beyond their capital base. If they borrow prudently they mostly absorb the risk themselves. But if they are allowed to borrow foolishly they impose the risk on others, the firms they borrow from, or even the entire society. Governments persistently strive to leverage their assets—political, financial, military—beyond their means at the expense of others.

In 1929 there were more than 24,000 banks operating in the United States. By the end of 1933 more than 9,000 of those banks had failed. Some of those 9,000 banks were "really" broke. Some were fundamentally sound but forced down by panicked depositors pulling their money out. And in 1929, the people primarily charged with determining the soundness of the banks were bank depositors, some large but mostly solidly middle-class Mom-and-Pops who ran the general store or the feed 'n grain.

When New Dealers tried to set up a banking system immune to panic, their top priority was to remove Mom-and-Pop from their role as bank police. The New Dealers created FDIC deposit insurance so depositors would be more comfortable leaving their deposits in the bank during times of crisis, which in turn would allow the banks to keep lending, supporting the whole credit system and thus the dollar itself. The New Dealers also strengthened the Federal Reserve's power to pump liquidity into the banking system, facilitating its role as "lender of last resort." This, too, was not only to protect banks or depositors but the people and businesses to whom banks lend money.

Expanding the federal safety net increased federal regulators' power to step in and close banks that strayed from the path of righteousness. With these steps the New Dealers believed they had created a circuit breaker to prevent isolated problems from becoming general banking panics. Mom-and-Pop depositor lost power to the government but gained protection, as did the banks' borrowers.

For many decades under the New Deal system everyone knew who the banks were and what the government had guaranteed. In recent decades, however, both Republicans and Democrats have supported an enormous expansion of the banking system beyond its New Deal limits. Democrats tended to do this in Democrat ways and Republicans tended to do it in Republican ways, but the push for bigger, and looser, banking was as bipartisan a cause as any in our lifetimes. As the banking system grew, the government persistently refused to accept the responsibilities of that growth. It broke the New Deal. It wanted the power the New Deal gave it over the banks, but it did not want to pay the price.

Left to their own devices, banks tend to be crabby and cautious with their money; those that aren't tend to die quick and painful deaths. Governments don't like crabby, cautious, or, for that matter, independent banks. Governments like banks that are free and easy with their money and responsive to the government's desires. Governments prefer loose credit to tight credit, and best of all they like loose credit extended to government's friends and pet projects, such as expanding home ownership. Most of all, the U.S. government wanted to achieve all this without paying for it, or at least without paying cash. Strategic ambiguity, implying government patronage and protection for loose banks and quasi-banks without actually putting up any money, was the government's way to do it on the cheap.

Fannie and Freddie offer perhaps the most obvious example. The twins were a crucial element in the government's push for expanded home ownership. The twins could finance that expansion only because of the government's implicit but ultimately ambiguous backing for the twins' bonds, which allowed the twins to borrow almost as cheaply as the government. The government would not, however, explicitly guarantee the twins bonds, a move that would have vastly increased the national debt, enraging voters.

Today there are perhaps $7 trillion dollars in old-style bank deposits in the banking system, about two-thirds of them FDIC-insured. Outside this "real" banking system are several trillion dollars more that look and feel a lot like bank deposits but aren't. The bulk of this is in "money market funds."

Money market funds, like banks, promise to have your cash available on demand. They are not insured by the government. Thus to keep the confidence of depositors they invest far more conservatively than banks, which are insured. A lot of money market fund deposits are reinvested into Treasury bills. Much also goes into those senior bonds issued by Fannie and Freddie that are implicitly, but not explicitly, guaranteed by the U.S. government. Such bonds are called "agencies" because although they are not Treasury paper they are issued by institutions acting as agents of the government. A cynic might conclude that the government has encouraged the growth of money market funds partly because as uninsured banks the funds have little alternative to putting their depositors' money into the debt of the government and its minions. Investing in government and quasi-government securities is a way of making these noninsured banks look like they are effectively backed by the government. This natural inclination is supported by the law, which, by setting severe restrictions on the type and amount of corporate bonds in which the money market funds can invest, effectively steers the funds toward government and "agency" debt.

So money market funds, quasi-banks, buy vast quantities of Fannie and Freddie bonds with their quasi-guarantee from Uncle Sam.

Except it's not quite that simple. For a variety of reasons, though your money market fund wants to invest in the twins' bonds, it does not *really* want to own them outright.[88] So the fund "buys" some of the bonds from, say, Merrill Lynch but with an agreement that Merrill will buy them back at a set price in a day, a week, a month, or some other short period.

Practically speaking, this means the money market fund has lent money to Merrill using the twins' paper as collateral.

The "overnight" money market comprising this trade and all sorts of variations thereof is called the "repo" market (for "repurchase"). It is enormous, running to trillions of dollars, though no single standard statistic exists to measure it. It is a pillar of the modern financial system, providing liquidity for commercial and investment banks, brokerages, hedge funds, and of course money market funds. It links the fate of all those entities together, those included in the New Deal banking system and those excluded from it.

Investment firms like Merrill and Bear and Lehman absolutely depend on this short-term credit market for their operating capital. Without that cash, they could not function. They could not, for instance, lend to their own customers who buy securities on credit. If, say, Merrill lost access to the overnight money market, it would be forced to pull credit from its own customers, who in turn would be forced to sell their own holdings. Such massive forced sales helped drive the crash in September 2008.

If Bear or Lehman or Merrill or Morgan Stanley or Citicorp lose access to the repo market, they become pariahs. Neither their creditors nor their customers will do business with them. And although access to the repo market is routine under ordinary circumstances, it does not take much going wrong to get shut out. In troubled times, a firm like Bear can lose access to the repo market simply because of a rumor that it is about to lose access, which is more or less what caused the firm to collapse in March of 2008.

The parts of the banking system that lie outside the New Deal structure are often called the "shadow" banking system. But this shadow is no phantom. It is neither insubstantial nor, as is often implied, unregulated. Every player is governed by one or more agencies of both federal and state governments. The biggest players, the bank holding companies that own both commercial and investment banks, have multiple masters, the most important being the Federal Reserve, the SEC, and the FDIC. Fannie and Freddie were governed by a notoriously weak regulatory agency but were under the very direct eye of Congress. It is true, as many observers have pointed out, that many of the banks, shadow or not, legally evaded certain regulations, including limits on how much they could borrow against or "leverage" their investment portfolios. They did this by carrying those investments in "off-balance-sheet," "Special Investment Vehicles." But this was hardly a secret. The Special Investment Vehicles were fundamental to the "structured" mortgage securities market. The regulators were all perfectly well aware of this practice and did nothing to discourage it.

During the crisis and the aftermath, any number of commentators could be heard to claim that the system was created by "deregulation," specifically the repeal of the Glass–Steagall Act under President Clinton. (Glass–Steagall had forbidden commercial banks from getting into the investment banking business, playing on Wall Street, etc.) The truth is closer to the opposite. Far from a "deregulation," the erosion and eventual repeal of Glass–Steagall gave the government more control over the shadow banking system by bringing more of the investment banking business effectivly into the Federal Reserve system. Repealing Glass–Steagall may have vastly increased the destructive potential of companies like Citigroup, but that potential was more firmly under the government's thumb than ever.

In any event, the argument over whether banks should be more or less regulated, even the suggestion that banks can ever be truly "deregulated" has always struck us as completely missing the point. In a modern financial system banks are agents of the government. The supposedly "odd" half-public, half-private arrangement that Fannie and Freddie had was odd only in that the twins were explicitly acknowledged as agencies. Banks, like lawyers (who are officers of the court), are licensed distributors of a government service. One of the government's jobs is to do justice; practically speaking lawyers are the allocators and distributors of that justice. They have monopoly access to the government's "justice distribution channels." Banks (shadow or not) play a similar role in the financial system. Like the provision of justice, establishing and regulating a currency is a government service. Banks are the licensed agents though which that service is performed.

Even in a banking system with few apparent regulations, the government remains the most powerful player if only because the government is always the banks' biggest customer, by orders of magnitude. Moreover, the single most important factor in any bank's business is the change in the price of money, the interest rate. Hundreds of thousands of pages have been written about the S&L collapse in the late 1980s and early 1990s, comprising endless arguments over who did what to whom. Most of that literature is irrelevant. When the government permitted the hyperinflation of the late 1970s and the double-digit interest rates that went with it, it destroyed the S&Ls by that single act. Institutions that had lent money long term in mortgages with single-digit interest rates could not long survive a double-digit regime. How the death scene played out over the next decade was merely a matter of detail. It's always like that. The question is never whether the government will control the banks but how badly it will muck up the job.

Under the current system the fates of the shadow institutions, the commercial "New Deal" banks, and the dollar itself are inextricably linked. A massive failure of the investment banks, for instance, would imperil the money market funds. (When Lehman collapsed in September 2008, one of the oldest money market funds, the Reserve Primary Fund, actually had to "break the buck," inform its investors that their dollars on deposit were now worth only 97 cents.) Any weakness in money market funds could (and did) cause a run on those funds, sending cash to the mattresses and drying up credit for the nation's businesses, threatening many with bankruptcy.

During the crisis and since, we have repeatedly heard the phrase "too big to fail." The phrase is often used vaguely, but "too big to fail" has a very specific meaning. A financial organization is too big to fail if its collapse could cause a massive withdrawal of dollars from credit markets, in turn triggering a massive deflation, a rise in the price of the dollar so great as to threaten mass bankruptcies.

This is not the place for a treatise on "fractional reserve banking." In brief, the number of dollars in effective circulation depends not mostly on the (relatively small) number of actual dollar bills abroad but on how those dollars are multiplied through the credit system. Tom has $10, lends $9 to Dick, and gets an IOU in return. Dick now lends $8 to Harry and gets an IOU from him. Assuming everyone has enough faith—enough credit—in those IOUs to treat them just like cash, instead of the $10 in circulation we started with, we now have $27. If everyone loses faith, if credit collapses, that extra $17 will disappear, and every enterprise, every loan supported by that $17, will be endangered. The money supply will drop overnight by roughly two-thirds. Money to fund businesses will become almost three times as hard to find and interest rates will nearly triple, which is just about what happened after September 15, 2008.

We apologize for going all "Finance 101" on you, but this little exercise does yield some insight into "too big to fail." Preserving the value of the dollar, avoiding both hyperinflation and catastrophic deflation is one of the government's core duties, written right down in the Constitution (c.f. "regulate the Value thereof"). Any institution the disorderly collapse of which would prevent the government from keeping the dollar stable is rightly considered too big to fail. This does not mean the government is obliged to "bail out" the offender. Summary execution is a fine and venerable option. But the government is absolutely obliged to keep the offender's collapse from destroying credit markets and thus the currency of the United States. The banking system, including the shadow banking system, is the mechanism through which the currency of the United States is created, circulated, and regulated in value. The government has an absolute responsibility to preserve that mechanism in working order.

As of the fall of 2007, the government had no announced policy as to how it would meet this obligation should the shadow system begin to fail, or even how it regarded behemoths like Citigroup that had a big foot in both the shadow and New Deal systems. The government continued to rely on strategic ambiguity. It simultaneously encouraged citizens to believe everything was under control while fervently proclaiming it would not create a "moral hazard" by underwriting the risks taken by banks, shareholders, and creditors. The government fooled no one, but confused everyone. Everyone knew the government would eventually do something to ward off collapse; no one knew what that would be. Strategic ambiguity did not lighten the government's load.

That load grew with every procrastination. Strategic ambiguity simply denied markets information.

Economics and politics are not physics, but both submit to something like the law of conservation of energy. Having deferred for so long the fair price of the power the government gained from the expanded banking system, eventually the government would have to pay that price with interest or lose control of the situation. Ultimately it would do both.

The government achieved expanded home ownership by allowing the mortgage market to become a subset of the securities-underwriting industry, long the core competence of the investment banks. This is what "securitization" and "structured finance" mean. But the mortgage market, along with the commercial loan market (which had also been "securitized") had long been the bedrock of the regular New Deal commercial banking system. The New Deal had guaranteed the safety of "real" banks not only to protect depositors but to protect the parties to which depositors' money was lent: homeowners and businesses. When the government allowed the mortgage market to be funded primarily by sources other than FDIC-insured deposits, it broke the New Deal and re-exposed mortgages (and securitized commercial loans) to the potential for market panic.

A homeowner with a 3-year, adjustable-rate mortgage has only three possible futures: sell, refinance, or mail back the keys. With the "depositors" (investors in mortgage-backed securities) ripping their money out of the mortgage market in the equivalent of a bank run, and AAA mortgage-backed bonds being tossed like toilet paper on Halloween, the "sell" and "refinance" options vanished: Mortgage terms, too easy but a few months before, tightened dramatically, turning ever more home"owners" into foreclosure statistics in an accelerating downward cycle.

By stretching its power beyond its purse or its competence, the government had lost control over not only the mortgage market but the entire banking system.

What should the government have done, in late summer of 2007, when it became clear that the collapsing market value of mortgage-backed securities was driving the entire banking system to the edge of catastrophe?

First, acknowledge the truth. Say right out loud that there is no shadow banking system, just a banking system. The government, with extraordinary regulatory authority over every institution involved had not only permitted but actively encouraged banks not covered by New Deal safeguards to play roles explicitly assigned to New Deal banks. An institution integral to maintaining dollar stability, an institution that extends credit to homeowners and secured business borrowers, and whose withdrawal of such credit could collapse credit markets, is a bank in the New Deal sense, no matter what it's called.

The political fallout of declaring Fannie, Freddie, and every major investment bank part of the New Deal system would have been huge. Outraged screams of moral hazard would have been heard everywhere. But the moral hazard had been created long before. By refusing to take this step government was not avoiding moral hazard; it was simply refusing to acknowledge what it had already done.

A declaration that everything that looks like a bank is a bank would have had some immediate implications. Under the New Deal arrangement, FDIC-insured, Federal Reserve member banks are explicitly under the supervision and ultimately the control of the U.S. government. Citizens are entitled to assume that as long as such a bank keeps its doors open it bears the imprimatur of the U.S. government. When the threat to these banks became apparent the government had an absolute obligation to determine for itself and its citizens their true financial conditions.

At a minimum, no later than the fall of 2007, the government should have asserted its supervision of all the major banks including the investment banks, determined as well as possible the value of their portfolios, reported those values to the public, and seized and closed in an orderly fashion banks that were beyond saving. It had abundant regulatory authority to do this, not to mention criminal bank fraud statutes that could have been brought to bear.

The government did not do any of this, in part because it still clung to the notion that public financial markets were the appropriate institutions to determine, say, the value of the mortgage-backed securities on a bank's balance sheet, and thus the solvency of the bank. In less than a year it would be forced to abandon this view under the most painful circumstances. But in one sense the government was right. It had yielded control over the banking system back to financial markets, back, in fact, to Mom-and-Pop, though now in the guise of the managers of Mom-and-Pop's 401Ks and corporate pension plans. And Mom-and-Pop were selling mortgage securities, directly and indirectly, in effect staging a run on the banks whose capital eroded with every decline in the market price of those securities.

So then, what to do? Actually there was a market-based solution open to the government. Markets process information. The chief defect of securities markets is that they are information impoverished. So give them the information.

The government should have made the banks—investment banks, commercial banks, all the banks on the too-big-to-fail list—publish their investment positions. In detail: lists of every security or derivative held in their portfolios, along with all data about the underlying mortgage pools, defaults so far, etc.

The banks would have screamed bloody murder about being forced to let competitors see what they owned. Nonsense. Investors who hold interesting or unusual positions in their portfolios may have something to lose by sharing such information—though less than is usually supposed. We at Whitebox would be quite happy to trade in a market in which all investors were obliged to publish their positions monthly, weekly, daily, hourly, or instantaneously. We think we would do better in such a market.

Banks, however, should have no such concerns about privacy. Banks that are too big to fail have no business taking "interesting" positions. Banks are not supposed to be extra clever; they are supposed to be extra careful. As it happens, we have never met a clever banker; now all the world knows we haven't many careful ones either.

Here's our suggestion for the new, new deal. Any financial institution whose failure would threaten U.S. credit markets,[89] impairing the government's ability to maintain a stable dollar, henceforth falls under the loving supervision and protection of the U.S. government. But since the government hasn't actually turned out to be very good at supervising even New Deal banks, it gets help. Every investor, every human being in the whole world gets to see the too-big-to-fail banks' investment portfolios.

Some discretion would be required with regard to the banks' traditional direct investments—individual mortgages or commercial loans—in order to protect the privacy of the borrowers. But in the case of tradable securities there is no excuse for any concealment.

Would it have done any good to publish this information in 2007, given how complicated were the relationships between the suspect securities and the defaulting mortgages? Almost certainly. We have harped on the opacity of the mortgage-backed securities at some length in this book. It was a huge problem. But it was a glass half-empty, glass half-full sort of problem. It was a huge problem not because the mortgage securities were utterly opaque but because a bank's investments really do need to be utterly transparent. A financial institution operating on capital reserves of pennies to the dollar, leveraged to 15 times its capital (or 30 or more using off-balance-sheet vehicles) can safely invest only in the most readily valued assets. Banks can't afford to invest in complex assets, the value of which is hard to verify in moments of crisis. Any doubt at all about the assets held by a bank leveraged thirty to one is a glass not just half empty but drained dry.

The world, thankfully, is full of investors who aren't like banks, who can take their time picking through the garbage, buying complexity and opacity and transforming them with due analysis and the passage of time into simplicity and transparency. That is to say, the world is full of investors, like conservative hedge funds, that are structured to be able to stand against a market panic, which the banks, as of late 2006 or 2007, were not. If the banks had been forced to open their books in 2007, the rag pickers of the financial world would have come forth in droves. Undoubtedly they would have turned up some news embarrassing to both the banks and to the government. But just as certainly they would have found good news as well and separated some sheep from some goats.

The government did just the opposite. When matters really started to deteriorate in September 2008, almost the first thing the government did was to try to silence the short sellers on the bizarre theory that the bad news would go away if no one talked about it. Undoubtedly the short sellers were playing rumors. But whose fault was it that rumors were all they had? When the crash came, the government would pour money into banks no longer capable of using it effectively to fight the panic. But it would encourage or allow those same banks to cut off credit from hedge funds and other investors willing to buy securities being dumped at fire-sale prices.

Capitalism demands the assumption that more and better information is preferable to less and worse. Perhaps by uncovering the reality of the banks' balance sheets in 2007 the government would have done even more damage to the economy than it ultimately did. But the assumption must run the other way. To presume that deceit and dissembling is the better policy is to give up on capitalism altogether.

CHAPTER FOURTEEN

Insolvent Immunity

T hroughout the latter part of 2007 and through the early months of 2008, the major players, especially the governments of the major economic powers, repeatedly described the looming crisis as one of "liquidity." Markets were nervous, and that was making cash a bit hard to come by. But, said reassuring voices, this is the sort of problem that the central banks of the world deal with all the time. In August of 2007 the major central banks grouped together to pump some $260 billion into the global credit system, which they do essentially by buying bonds from client banks, which then use the resulting cash inflows as reserves against which to make additional loans. To the same end, the U.S. Federal Reserve cut its interest rates by a half point, a bolder move than its usual 25 basis points, to make it easier for the big banks to borrow. In early September the Fed pumped another $31 billion into U.S. money markets. Over the next year the Fed would take increasingly drastic steps to insure the financial system had dollars to spare.

None of these were bad things to do. Almost all panics do become crises of liquidity. But a mere shortage of cash is never the heart of the matter. At its core a panic is a crisis of information. Danger lurks, but those threatened do not know precisely what the danger is or how to cope with it. The answer to panic is information—if it comes early enough. But information is hard, and (for governments) money is easy. Money is what they've got. In particular, pumping money more or less aimlessly into the banks is easier than telling the truth about them or even finding out what the truth is.

For a while, for longer even than we expected, markets seemed to buy the story. But ultimately in an atmosphere of deceit, with information in desperately short supply, trust evaporated, markets ceased to function, and we ended up with a full-blown panic. A true panic destroys liquidity faster than the government can provide it because the cash the government hands out gets hidden in the mattress rather than entered into the credit system.

To see why both the governments and the banks were tempted to portray the crisis as being about liquidity, leave securities markets aside for a moment. Think instead about the three basic bad things that can happen to a business.

The most basic bad thing is that a business can be unprofitable. A business that never makes a profit is doomed. But most good businesses can survive being unprofitable for a while. Over the long term, nothing is worse for a business than to be unprofitable. In the near term, it may be just a phase.

The second bad thing that can happen to a business is that it can be insolvent; its liabilities can be worth more than its assets. It can owe more than it owns. This, too, can be fatal. If the wrong people—like creditors or bankers—find out that a business is insolvent, the company will be busted a lot quicker than if the same people find out it is momentarily unprofitable. Mitigating this danger, it can be hard to determine if a company is solvent. Most of the time, nobody—not even the owners—knows for sure exactly what a company's assets are worth. Many businesses, including banks, go through moments when only God knows whether the business is "really" insolvent. The moment passes, the firm lives to fight another day. Insolvency is more immediately dangerous than unprofitability, if anyone finds out. But often no one does.

Finally, there is illiquidity. You can have a great business, make money, own more than you owe—and still not have any cash. Now at first this might not seem so bad. Which sounds worse—being broke or not being able to find an ATM machine? But a lack of cash is hard to hide and can kill very quickly. Perfectly good businesses do die of illiquidity. They can run out of cash to operate even though their operations are profitable. They can run out of cash even though they are solvent. Their assets might really be worth twice their liabilities, but they can't turn those assets into cash quickly enough to pay their bills.

So illiquidity is dangerous. But it is also eminently solvable—all you need is a bank or a government willing to lend. This we always have in modern central banking systems. If governments can persuade markets that something like the mortgage crisis is merely a crisis of liquidity, it has in effect persuaded them it is readily solvable.

Then there is the moral dimension. If a business finds itself in trouble because it has invested badly, or has a bad business model, or has been cooking the books or covering for those who have (three out of four being almost certainly true of every important player in the mortgage debacle), it's difficult to persuade the average voter—or policeman—that the responsibility lies anywhere but with the owners or managers of the firm, or with those who were supposed to be watching them, like Congress or the Whitehouse. Going broke "for real" has moral implications, which is why bankruptcy used to be considered shameful.

Illiquidity is a different matter. Illiquidity can be morally ambiguous. Everyone has heard of perfectly sound businesses running short of cash. Everyone has heard stories of meritorious startups that ran out of money before they hit pay dirt. The moral of such stories is always that it was the tightfisted moneymen, not the would-be entrepreneurs, who were shortsighted. Illiquidity can almost always be blamed on someone else.

Most people can imagine running short of cash due to unexpected events, even if they have behaved prudently and uprightly. As the old Green Bay Packers used to say, "We never lose, but some days we run out of time." Illiquidity, one faintly senses, can be an act of God, or at least of those lesser and more mischievous deities, the market gods. Illiquidity can be "not our fault."

When government steps in to solve a crisis of liquidity, by supplying some, no one shouts "moral hazard." Maintaining the stability of the currency, avoiding both inflation and deflation, is clearly a job for the government. No one supposes that correctly maintaining the value and supply of the dollar is a corrupt enterprise. By contrast, failed businesses are saved by "bailouts," an ugly word and an ugly thing. Automobile companies get bailed out— and airlines, speaking of ugly. As events would show, the last thing the government wished was to appear to be bailing out the banks. Everything would be so much better, so much less judgmental, if it could all be treated as a matter of liquidity.

It was a lie, and it struck deep in the heart of capitalism.

Here is the quickest way to determine whether you are operating in an honest capitalist system or a corrupt imitation thereof: check the bankruptcy rates. For most of the last hundred years, the United States has had both the strongest economy and the highest bankruptcy rate of any reasonably large developed nation. By contrast, the old Soviet Union had a bankruptcy rate of essentially zero. Many state-owned enterprises were organized to function like businesses. They had managers and employees, bought materials, made and sold products. But none of them ever went broke.

And that told the whole story. Socialism, the socialists say, has never really been tried. And in a way that is true. The Soviet Union was not a socialist economy so much as it was a crony-capitalist economy. The Soviet government loved the nation's businesses so much that it would never let them fail. The crucial mechanism for this failure rate of zero was an almost entirely fictitious currency, the ruble of infinite flexibility, endless liquidity, and minimal value to cover over the lies.

Every Soviet business manager was well stocked with excuses for not meeting quota, or even better, with a sheaf of dummied documents proving he had. The government had no impersonal mechanism to punish the inefficient. In order to shut down a failed state business, the government would have to (a) tell the truth, which would mean confessing the government's own mismanagement, and (b) take direct responsibility for things like layoffs, an unpleasant experience even for politicians who regularly get 99 percent of the vote. The ruble could paper over the problems.

A tour through the economies of old Europe—also more accurately described as crony capitalist than socialist—confirms the point. Low bankruptcy rate = chronic underperformance. Similarly, the essence of the Japanese malaise was the government's insistence on avoiding outright bank failures at almost any cost. A once-vibrant economy was crippled by the loss of an efficient mechanism for reallocating capital away from bad loans and failed enterprises.

When the S&L crisis struck in the late 1980s, the (GHW) Bush administration, to its credit, offered a largely capitalist response. Sure, there was a bailout of sorts, and depositors were protected from their own folly. But some banks were closed and some people did go to jail—sometimes even the right banks and the right people. Bush did not help the S&Ls paper over the whole thing or subject the country to endless reruns of Banks of the Living Dead.

As the mortgage crisis unfolded it soon became clear that a different Bush was in charge. As late as the spring of 2008, only the Bear "hedge funds" and a bunch of mortgage originators had been allowed to die. No institution with any prestige or political clout went under. Even Countrywide was saved by Bank of America, using cheap, laundered cash from Uncle Sam. The government had neither seized and shuttered any banks nor taken responsibility for determining whether the banks were actually solvent. Governments not only here but throughout the world remained utterly passive except for one thing—they all agreed to hand out cheap cash to the banks that had created the problem.

To blame a mere shortage of cash for the evils caused by incompetence and corruption is the favorite lie of socialists and crony capitalists everywhere. Socialists always say there is no problem of inequality or poverty that can't be solved with cash. It is cash alone that separates the rich from the poor—not talent or skill or hard work or thrift. Similarly, in the socialist view it is only access to capital that separates "greedy" and "monopolistic" (read "successful") firms from the thousand flowers that would bloom if only the government would create a "level playing field" and "enforce competition."

After the socialists become the government and begin evolving into crony capitalists, their favored beneficiaries—Soviet state-owned factories, Japanese banks, Fannie and Freddie in the United States—are always described as faultlessly devoted, idealistic, and hardworking, or at least essential. If they underperform (and they always underperform), it is only because they are short of cash—which the government then always provides in some form or other.

As the mortgage crisis unfolded, the government could have used its cash to buy time to assert its authority over the big banks and get to the truth. That's what the New Deal system is supposed to do. Instead the government almost randomly pumped liquidity into the system in the apparent hope that the truth would never come out. Far from providing markets with information, the government sought "insolvent immunity" for holders of suspect assets to cover over their incompetence and fraud with cheap cash.

Above all, as 2007 dragged on into 2008, no one of any significance went to jail. There was no serious inquiry as to whether any of the major players had suborned bank fraud, for instance, by funding hundreds of billions in "liars' loans." As we wrote at the time:

> No one will go to jail. Merrill and Citi and the rest will escape the fate they deserve. The government will . . . punish the honest to save the cheaters. The crooks cry for liquidity and the government by all indications plans to give it to them. . . .We have rejoined the economy of the lie and we will get what liars deserve.

Throughout 2007 and early 2008, the government pointed a fire hose of liquidity at the economy, apparently hoping the money would support the mortgage market. But people who have just been badly burned in one sector do not soon go back, even with free money. They put their free money somewhere else. When the government pumped money into the economy after the tech wreck, the money did not flow back into tech. Tech share prices, irrationally high for several years, stayed irrationally low for several years. Much of the money went into the housing market, one bubble replacing another. As the government opened up the gusher in 2007, the money did not go back into housing or mortgage-backed securities. It went into oil and commodities and even the stock market, with the Dow hitting an all-time high in October of 2007, just as the banks were beginning to crack.

So much money did the Fed pour out, so eager was every politician in Washington to "stimulate" that we made a fairly serious error. We were sure Treasury paper would suffer from the overload, so we began to bet against it. What we did not grasp was how the government, by responding to an information crisis with funds rather than facts, would eventually create an environment so terrifying that Treasury paper—no matter how much the government printed—would look rock solid compared to everything else. By feeding panic in the real economy, the government boosted its own bonds. Ultimately when the crisis became the crash, private credit would almost disappear while Treasuries soared in value.

The government fell into the same deeply anti-capitalist error that plagues contemporary financial theory: it put money before mind. Rather than addressing the intellects of citizens with the information to make prudent decisions, it tried to bribe them with cash to make foolish ones. It tried to restore confidence, without confiding. It asked people to trust, without allowing them to verify.

CHAPTER FIFTEEN

Black September

In March 2008, the great silence was split by a thundercrack as Bear Sterns collapsed. Bad as that news was, there was a silver lining. After months of inaction and dissembling, it seemed that the government might actually be getting on track. To deal with Bear the government imposed swiftly a result that plausibly might have come from a dangerously drawn-out bankruptcy proceeding. The shareholders, recently owners of a $150 stock, were cut down to $10, paid by JP Morgan. Bondholders, and preferred equity holders, were preserved with the help of a $29 billion loan from the Fed to Morgan. Crucially the deal also protected "counterparties": customers and creditors, including other banks, whose cash or securities were in Bear's custody at the time it was shutdown. If counterparties had been unable to collect swiftly, the shut down of Bear could have set off a chain reaction of collapse throughout the system.

Strictly speaking, "counterparties" are simply two parties to a contract or transaction. But in finance, counterparties is the term we use especially to describe the institutions that sustain transactions in a credit economy. Banks are the easiest example. If Bob employs Bill and writes him a paycheck every week, and Joe is the grocer with whom Bill shops, paying by bankcard or check, then

Bob and Bill and Joe are the parties to the various transactions. The counterparty is the Main Street Bank where they all keep their checking accounts. Before dealing with each other, Bob and Bill and Joe all consider each other's creditworthiness. That's normal. But they don't usually stop to think about whether the Main Street Bank might go bust before completing their transactions. And that's a good thing. Because if Bob, Bill, or Joe had to worry about whether the bank could complete transactions among the three of them, business would cease.

In a modern economy no transaction requiring credit—even overnight, even for an instant of time—is possible without trusted counterparties. Without counterparties even currency begins to disappear because so much of our "currency" is simply an entry on some counterparty's books. It is pointless to pump money into an economy in which the biggest, most commonly used counterparties are thought to be at risk. If everyone senses inordinate risk, everyone will horde cash. Flooding the economy with dollars will not recreate lost trust; currency cannot substitute for credibility. By acting swiftly to shut down Bear in an orderly way and guaranteeing the transactions of those who used Bear as a counterparty, the government signaled that it grasped what was at stake. It came very late in the game, but it was the right move.

It was widely assumed by investors that the Bear deal had established a rough pattern for future government action in the crisis. Imperiled institutions, even "shadow banks," would be swiftly shuttered rather than allowed to become dangerous dominoes. Common shareholders would be executed or at least tortured just as in real bankruptcies. Meanwhile, counterparties, bondholders, and preferred "shareholders" (really just junior bondholders, despite the name) would be protected for the sake of market order. Most strikingly, in the wake of Bear's collapse the government gave the Federal Reserve some power to act as lender of last resort to investment banks even though they were not members of the Federal Reserve. The government was still mumbling and miming rather than boldly proclaiming a policy, but the message seemed clear enough. The government seemed to be resolving some of its "strategic ambiguity."

Then came the Fannie and Freddie spectacle and the government surrendered all its credibility in a matter of hours.

On July 13, 2008, Treasury Secretary Paulson announced that the government was taking action to shore up the finances of the twins based on existing statutory authority. At Paulson's urging, Congress swiftly followed up with the Housing and Economic Recovery Act of 2008, which the president signed on July 30. This created a new, far more powerful regulatory authority to oversee the twins. More important in the eyes of the market, the act empowered Treasury to lend the twins funds to keep them afloat, limited apparently only by the debt ceiling of the U.S. Treasury, which was duly raised by $800 billion.

After this first bailout, government swore up and down that the twins were solid as a rock. "What's important are facts," proclaimed Sen. Christopher Dodd, chairman of the relevant Senate committee, on CNN, "and the facts are that Fannie and Freddie are in sound situation. . . . They have more than adequate capital. They're in good shape." Secretary Paulson with perhaps a finer sense of the need to preserve deniability proclaimed, "Their regulator has made clear they are adequately capitalized."[90]

As CEO of Goldman Sachs, Paulson had been deeply involved with the twins. Now he went so far as to call leading investment bankers to urge them to buy Fannie's bonds, prompting former Fed governor Lawrence Lindsey to remark, "Things are somewhat amiss when a country's finance minister plays bond salesman for a supposedly privately owned company."[91]

In May, just two months before the July bailout, Fannie and

Freddie had announced new issues of preferred stock. Not really "stock," preferred shares are more accurately described as junior bonds that carry a dividend that must be paid before any payments are made to common shareholders. Unlike the big investment banks solicited by Secretary Paulson to buy the twins' senior bonds, for the preferred issue many of the buyers were state-chartered or smaller federal banks for which propping up the twins was something between an act of public service and (they hoped) enlightened self-interest. They would soon learn to regret their public spiritedness.

Prices on the twins' preferred shares had slumped badly in early summer. After the July bailout and the government's ringing endorsement of the twins' health, they recovered somewhat. Acting on the government's assurances, investors who had been wary of the twins' preferreds began to buy. We bought some ourselves. Fools.

On September 7—less than two months after the government publicly gave the twins an open-ended claim on its checkbook and the Treasury secretary had been pimping their bonds—the government declared Fannie and Freddie hopeless as private entities, seized them, and placed them in "conservatorship." The terms were different from the Bear seizure, however. Senior bondholders, including those old colleagues Secretary Paulson had been pitching, were held harmless. But unlike Bear's preferred shareholders who had been protected by the government in the Bear collapse, the twins' preferred shareholders, who only weeks before had been told by the government that the twins were solid as a rock, saw their dividends canceled.

The U.S. government, with access to information no private investor could summon, had lured investors into a trap. To a market urgently in need of information, the government had supplied disinformation. Had the CEO of a private company gone about telling investors that his company had "more than adequate capital" and was in a "sound situation" knowing that the company might be in bankruptcy within weeks, he would have gone to jail for securities fraud. Although the collapse of Lehman a few days later would actually provoke the crash, the government's Fannie and Freddie con probably made it inevitable.

Government honchos excused their actions by saying that, given the depth of the current crisis, they could not justify extending taxpayer money to the twins (which they had agreed to do only weeks before) without seizing control. The implications of this were huge. The government's statements could only mean the mortgage-backed securities that dominated the twins' portfolios were so weak that the twins were beyond saving. The obvious implication was that the mortgage debt on the books of the nation's banks could bring them down as well.

But hadn't we already known that? Not really. The whole world knew there was trouble afoot. We all knew the market had been savagely marking down AAA mortgage paper. But none of the government's actions to this point had suggested that banks heavily concentrated in such mortgage paper were thereby doomed. To the contrary, if there were doomed member banks out there, why hadn't they been shut down? The government has absolute, transparent access to the books of the banks. That it had left them standing had been taken as a powerful signal that the crisis, though painful, was well short of catastrophe. Now the government, with that same access to the twins' financials, had declared them unsalvageable, implying the banks might be as well.

Suddenly the government's actions seemed to establish two points. First there must be a very large but unquantified deficit, exceeding even the massive write-downs so far, on the books of many crucial but unnamed banks. This was not unlike telling a clutch of children huddled around a campfire, "There are big bad bogeymen out in the dark but we can't tell you how big, how bad, how many, or where."

Furthermore, by encouraging investors to buy the twins' preferred issues and then punishing investors who did so the government told the children, "It would be very brave and good of you to go out and fight the bogeymen. But if you do, we might change sides in the middle and help them eat you."

Next came Lehman Bros., which, subject to rumors that it could not raise cash and would soon be shut out of the repo market, teetered on the edge in early September. Now the government changed the rules again. A major financial intermediary, counterparty to billions in transactions across global markets, a major player in the repo market, holding large stocks of cash from money market funds, was threatened by the panic the government had helped to create. Given the government's stated goal of keeping credit markets from seizing, and its previous behavior, including the way it had handled Bear and established a lender-of-last-resort fund for investment banks like Lehman, markets clearly expected the government to step in. The government flirted, and by flirting further weakened market confidence in Lehman. Then the government turned away, and Lehman collapsed.

As the *New York Times* reported, on the evening of Friday, September 12, future Treasury secretary Timothy Geithner, then-president of the New York Federal Reserve, flanked by Fed Chairman Bernanke, and Treasury Secretary Paulson "summoned the heads of major Wall Street firms to a meeting in Lower Manhattan and insisted" the banks, not the government, "rescue the stricken investment bank and develop plans to stabilize the financial markets." Geithner insisted that "an industry solution was needed, no matter what . . . and . . . that if the industry failed to solve the problem their individual banks might be next."[92]

According to the *Times*, the meeting included the heads of

Goldman Sachs, JPMorgan Chase, Morgan Stanley, Citigroup, Merrill Lynch, and others. But "Lehman Brothers was noticeably absent from the talks." As the *Times* noted, "Bank of America and two British banks, Barclays and HSBC, have expressed interest in bidding for Lehman Brothers," but only with the kind of support the government extended to JPMorgan to help it buy Bear Stearns.[93]

The government refused. "Mr. Paulson and Mr. Geithner made it clear to the company, its potential suitors, and to the meeting participants on Friday that the government has no plans to put taxpayer money on the line. The government is deeply worried that its actions have created a moral hazard and the Federal Reserve does not want to reach deeper into its coffers. Instead, Mr. Paulson and Mr. Geithner insist that Wall Street needs to come up with an industry solution . . ."[94]

Lehman was significantly larger than Bear Sterns and far more entwined as a counterparty throughout the banking system here and abroad. But, the *Times* reported, "Fed and Treasury officials were convinced that Lehman posed far fewer real risks than Bear Stearns had back in March," in part because since spring, regulators, including Federal Reserve officials, had been ensconced in the office of every major investment bank monitoring the banks' investments. "Fed and Treasury officials have also been taking the daily pulse of executives and traders on Wall Street for months" and with respect to Lehman detected "nothing near the panic that caused Wall Street executives to bombard Mr. Paulson with dire warnings about a Bear Stearns collapse in March." Fed officials "also saw few signs that fears about the future of the investment bank were spilling over to fears about its customers and trading partners."[95]

The government had publicly assumed vast responsibility for the investment banks, confirmed to every major player in the industry that it had assumed such responsibility by assigning teams of regulators to oversee the daily business of the investment banks. Then, despite this privileged access, the government misread the situation, fumbled the job, denied the responsibilities it had recently assumed, and walked away.

Lehman filed. Within days many of the securities it had been holding were sold off in a massive liquidation, helping drive prices toward the cellar. Counterparty assets were frozen, perhaps the worst possible result from the point of view of keeping credit markets—i.e., the nation's currency—functioning. The notions of currency and counterparty are inseparable. Without counterparties, markets are reduced to barter.

By this time the government had: (a) intimated that deficits in the financial sector were so large and widespread that "anyone could be next" (b) terrified private investors from making investments that might preserve the solvency of deteriorating institutions (c) assumed unprecedented responsibility for investment banks outside the Federal Reserve system and then abandoned that responsibility and (d) made clear that its policy would change on an ad hoc basis.

Later, Geithner, Paulson, and others repeatedly claimed that the government's bizarre behavior was necessary to avoid creating "moral hazard"—economic incentives that reward bad behavior. When an insurance company allows a million-dollar property to be insured for $10 million, it creates a moral hazard. When the government extended Fannie and Freddie hundreds of billions in credit, as it did in July, it created an incentive for Fannie to risk the government's money to make money for itself. Therefore, claimed the government, Fannie's preferred shareholders had to be punished when the firm was seized in September, otherwise investors would learn the bad lesson that by investing in the twins they could reap great rewards without accepting any risks. Lehman had to be allowed to collapse in order to reinforce the lesson.

This was nonsense several times over. In the first place, the way to avoid moral hazard is to not create it in the first place, not to arbitrarily punish some set of investors whose only crime was to take the government at its word—given only weeks before in the case of investors in the twins' preferred debt. That government regulators had been sitting in the offices of Lehman and others for months itself constituted a moral hazard, an implicit signal that the government was working round the clock to keep Lehman and the others from going off the rails.

More important is that the government always has at its disposal a perfect weapon with which to fend off moral hazard—the criminal law. The most efficient way to discourage moral hazard is for federal prosecutors to put crooked or negligent corporate officers in jail, not depend on markets to punish random shareholders.

The government's theory of moral hazard assumed that shareholders are real owners of the firm and actually responsible for management. This is ridiculous. The very idea of a moral act supposes voluntary action, which is notoriously beyond the reach of the shareholder. To assume that the buying and selling of shares amounts to managing the firm is the most extreme form of efficient market worship.

Efficient market idolatry and crony capitalism end up in the same place. The preference for public financial markets over all other markets creates a preference for weak ownership over strong. Crony capitalism thrives on weak owners, or at least dependent owners. The American progressive tradition of Teddy Roosevelt and Woodrow Wilson is the most frank and unapologetic articulation of the crony-capitalist outlook. It looks kindly on big business but only as part of the progressive dream of a grand alliance of big business, big labor, and big government governing society. Big business may look strong. But to the progressives, the leading American proponents of crony capitalism, the virtue of a big business is not its strength but the breadth of its reach. That breadth makes big business a meaningful member of the grand alliance—one handshake stands for many. But that breadth also makes it a dependable and dependent ally; government can always find a point of influence.

The crony capitalists prefer institutions over citizens; they will always prefer to push costs and blame onto a crowd of citizens rather than a committee of colleagues and allies. And so a crony-capitalist government will always prefer to punish—even defraud—unknown shareholders and investors rather than bring the guilty elite to account.

The government's public agonizing over the issue of moral hazard merely highlighted its amoral treatment of the crisis. The government's refusal to make moral judgments on a massive bank fraud was even more destructive than the refusal of modern investment theory to be "judgmental" about assets. The government was at every point as willing to punish the innocent—from shareholders to bondholders to taxpayers—as it was loath to punish the guilty. As Robert Novak pointed out in one of his last columns, on the day the Senate was considering the July 2008 bailout of Fannie and Freddie, it was not until well into the hearings with Secretary Paulson that any senator even bothered to ask whether the "well-paid officials and directors of the mortgage companies" should be held accountable.

Paulson's response, "I'm not looking for scapegoats."

On September 15 as Lehman declared bankruptcy, financial markets "seized." What did that mean? Overnight, nothing in the world except an actual dollar in your pocket could be relied upon to be worth a dollar. No funds "intermediated" by the credit system were guaranteed to be available. In the most extreme case, the Reserve Primary Fund, a money market fund with some $65 billion was forced to "break" the dollar. On Tuesday September 16, the managers of the Reserve fund had to tell shareholders that their one-dollar shares were currently worth only 97 cents. This was only the second time in history that a money fund had been forced to break the buck; the previous occasion had involved a small fund in 1994. The Reserve Primary Fund's problem? It had used Lehman as a counterparty in some transactions and at least briefly could not be sure of coming up with enough cash to cover withdrawals.

This was panic in its purest form. In a system in which a depositor cannot put $1 in his savings account without fear that it will shrink to 97 cents overnight, credit-based transactions become all but impossible. The imperative to hold cash and only cash becomes overwhelming. Lehman had been one of the largest issuers of short-term commercial credit in the world. When the government appeared to abandon Lehman without a struggle— even worse, when Paulson tried to downplay the importance of letting it go—markets had no sense of the rules or whether there were rules at all.

With Lehman's fall the U.S. commercial bond market began to disappear. Other money market funds began to see massive with-drawals. Money market funds, remember, specialize in very short-term, well-secured securities, including the short-term loans that businesses take out to provide daily operating cash for the busi-ness. Without that cash, even sound businesses could be swiftly crippled, which would mean their longer-term bonds could also go into default.

In this atmosphere, soon investors could not tell what their bond portfolios were worth because many bonds would not trade at any price. Within days it became possible to buy performing bonds—bonds still paying their coupons—for dimes and eventu-ally pennies on the dollar.

As yet unaware of how difficult the government planned to make it for investors to reboot credit markets, we greeted what we saw as "unprecedented opportunities." In one of his monthly letters to investors, Andy noted that in his previous thirty years in the business, he had rarely been able to buy performing bonds at less than 30 cents on the dollar, and never less than 20 cents. On one day that September, we did it twice, buying the performing bonds of one firm for 14 cents on the dollar, and another for a nickel.

A measure of how insane markets became: within a few days there was actually a market in "default swaps" for U.S. Treasury bonds. Yes, for some small fraction of a penny you could actually buy a dollar's worth of insurance against a default by the U.S. Treasury. We just scratched our heads. Who would pay out the claims, in what currency, and what would we do with the "money"? Who buys insurance against the end of the world?

CHAPTER SIXTEEN

Sucked into the Green Zone

On April 16 of 2009, after six months poised at the edge of the abyss, General Growth Properties filed for bankruptcy. There is no particular reason, gentle reader, for you to care about GGP except that its path to bankruptcy serves as a splendid illustration of the impact of the government's reaction to the crash and what happens to more-or-less sound companies in a general credit contraction.

GGP was a holding company for upscale shopping malls. It owned, for instance, the Water Tower in Chicago. GGP's income easily covered its interest obligations by a factor of somewhat more than 1.5, a strong indication the firm was solvent. It had a lot of debt but nothing unsustainable in the ordinary course of business: equity amounted to roughly 20 percent of total capital, that capital being upscale real estate. Another way of saying GGP had 20 percent equity is that it was leveraged five to one. By comparison, some of the nation's great banks were leveraged twenty or thirty to one against similar assets.

And yet an apparently healthy GGP was pushed into bankruptcy by senior creditors—mortgage holders in this case—suddenly eager to pounce and seize its assets. And that was the curious thing. Normally they would not have pounced. It is all but unheard of for a company to be forced into bankruptcy while current on its obligations and with 1.5X interest coverage.

So why did they do it? Simple. As credit markets crashed the cost of borrowing dollars—for most firms—tripled almost overnight and did not fall appreciably until well into 2009.

We are going to do just a little bit of math in a moment and many of you will hate that. So we'll give you the key principle before we do the math. If the cost of borrowing against an asset—like a car or a house or a shopping mall—triples, then all else being equal, the selling price of the asset must fall by two-thirds.

Say you buy a house for $300,000 when mortgage rates are 5 percent, making your annual payment around $15,000. If rates suddenly go up to 15 percent, you probably are not going to be able to sell the house for much more than $100,000, which will cost the new owner the same $15,000 a year that you were paying. The interest rate is the price of money. If the price of dollars goes up, the dollar price of the house must go down.

In the real world this does not work perfectly or instantly, but it's true enough to matter.

Here's the view of General Growth Properties from 30,000 feet. The company had purchased about $30 billion worth of shopping malls. These malls generated about $2 billion a year in cash before interest payments. To buy the malls GGP put down $6 billion of its own money and borrowed $24 billion at an average rate of about 5 percent. That meant the company had an interest cost of about $1.25 billion a year against $2 billion in rental income. That gave GGP a profit (before depreciation and taxes) of about $750 million on equity of $6 billion.

The debt, roughly three-quarters mortgages and one-quarter

corporate bonds, matured at a variety of dates up to ten years out. But in the fall of 2008, just as credit markets collapsed, some of that debt was about to come due. GGP had assumed it would be able to refinance the debt at roughly the same 5 percent at which it had borrowed originally. Then the crash came and it could not.

Because of the collapse of credit markets, by October 2008, only a federally supported bank (or one of the growing list of federally supported institutions under the government's bailout programs) could finance even top-shelf shopping malls at 5 percent.

At that point in the crisis the cost of money was so high that GGP would have had to pay something like 15 percent interest. Practically speaking, that would reduce the value of the shopping malls from $30 billion to about $10 billion.[96] Meanwhile, the mortgage holders had lent out $18 billion on assets that now appeared to be worth only $10 billion. Naturally they wanted to asset their rights as senior lenders and claim the entire property. So they pushed GGP into bankruptcy.

Since the bondholders are junior to the mortgage holders, in theory the bondholders might get nothing until the mortgage holders recovered all their money. With mortgage holders owed $18 billion on now $10 billion worth of property, the bonds of this recently solvent company were soon selling for less than a nickel on the dollar.

At that price, the bonds turned out to be a great investment: A nickel turned out to be simply a panic price. As everyone calmed down and realized that the bankruptcy judge was not going to give everything to the mortgage holders, creating a windfall from a sudden massive dollar deflation, the bonds began to recover. They were headed back toward par by the fall of 2009.

But why did it take so long? And why did the same thing happen to thousands of other similarly basically sound companies? The Merrill Lynch "distressed" bond index includes only bonds priced so low that their yield is more than a thousand basis points, or 10 percentage points over the yield on Treasuries. On March 1, 2007, that index included just 21 names. By March 1, 2009, it included almost 1,200 names.

But what about TARP (Troubled Relief Asset Program), and the $700 billion bailout, and all the acronyms to follow, and the Fed slashing rates, and the banks being stuffed to the gills with cash and promising in return to spread dollars throughout the land? Why wasn't that money getting to GGP and the thousands of other suddenly distressed firms?

As a colleague of ours pointed out at the time, the best possible analogy to the Bush administration's policy after the crash was that same administration's policy in Iraq from late 2003 up until 2007. Under that policy, symbolized by the infamous "Green Zone" in Baghdad, the government established a handful of areas nearly (though not quite) impenetrable to the insurgents, in which areas U.S. government operations, and especially the armed forces themselves, were based. When the insurgents struck outside the Green Zone, U.S. troops would massively deploy to punish them, after which our troops would return to their bases. The theory was that this strategy would keep the troops safe to sustain a strategy of wearing down the enemy until order could be restored to the country. The strategy not only failed to restore order, it cost the lives of several thousand American soldiers killed not only on the raids but going back and forth.

General David Petraeus identified and reversed the essential flaw in the strategy. This was the implicit assumption that an orderly, productive society can be established by dividing the country between small safe zones, created by massive and unsustainable government expenditures, and large barbarian zones encompassing the economy that must ultimately support the government and its best friends inside their gated community.

This cannot work. It is almost exactly what the Bush administration did in financial markets.

When a massive and sudden credit collapse hits a modern economy, borrowing becomes extremely expensive for everyone—almost. The government, and certain government-backed institutions—for instance, banks that have earned the government's special favor by imperiling the entire nation—will still be able to borrow at pre-deflation rates. With money plentiful and cheap on the government's side of the room, but scarce and expensive on the other side of the room, assets will flow toward the government's side like water flowing downhill. Over time all "normal" asset holders—those who, lacking the largesse of government, can borrow only at high rates—will lose everything they own to those who can borrow at the government rate. If government-backed entities can finance an asset at 5 percent, and everyone else in the room is obliged to finance it at 15 percent, and this goes on long enough, ultimately every asset in the economy will be owned by the government's pals.

Thus—just as in an inflation—in a sudden catastrophic deflation the government can massively confiscate assets from one group of citizens and shift them to another, or keep them for itself. At first this seems odd since the government is a massive debtor. Deflation is generally held to be bad for debtors, as inflation is generally held to be good for them. Is this not the very reason governments are tempted to inflate the currency so that their own debts can be wiped away, paid off with cheap currency of their own issuance?

All true. But the deflation of 2008—let us call it the deflation of the Red Zone—was not the result of a long-term shortage of currency (as, for instance, the United States saw frequently in the nineteenth century). It was the result of a catastrophic credit collapse. In such a collapse, the government, as the sole trusted agent in the midst of a financial terror, can borrow and lend at an extraordinarily favorable spread, putting assets on its balance sheet at amazing bargain prices. This is exactly what the government did. For months, the only borrower with access to credit on reasonable terms was the U.S. government and its minions. Because only the Treasury could borrow, only the Treasury or its protectorates could lend or buy.

If this condition could persist forever, ultimately only the state would own any assets. This is why the price of the bailout kept rising, why more firms kept going more broke, and the government had to create more and more money to shove into the banks and the car companies and whatever else. The government borrowed, lent, and bought in an attempt to keep the system afloat, but the spread between Green Zone and Red Zone interest rates would not close. Perversely, by driving down Treasury rates the government actually widened the spread. Normally, of course, lower Treasury rates bring lower commercial rates; spreads, not rates, rule the world. But in the panic that link was broken. Lower government rates had no gravitational effect outside the Green Zone because the money would not venture into the Red Zone almost no matter how high the reward. In a panic, everyone focuses on the undoubted truth that poor is better than dead. To see this, take a look at chart 6. For months as rates on Treasury paper fell, and as the Fed kept cutting rates for banks, interest rates paid by suddenly imperiled businesses continued to soar.

Thus for all the cheap money Treasury pumped out, it achieved little except extending the definition of the U.S. Treasury to include banks (and banks-elect), Fannie and Freddie, AIG, the auto companies, etc. An ever-expanding Green Zone of institutions was adopted by the Treasury because they had become a danger to themselves and others. All these, using government

CHART 6
The High Yield Spread
Merrill Lynch HY Index vs. 5-Year Treasury Yields

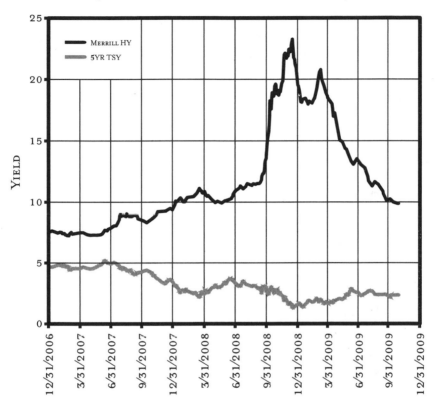

Source: Bloomberg

money, could finance assets at reasonable rates. Everyone else, the folks who before the crisis made money rather than lost it, acquired assets prudently, and did not recklessly imperil the nation's financial system, remained out in the cold, borrowing at high double-digit rates, or not at all.

Chart 6 shows two interest rates (technically "yields") on medium-term bonds. One is the rate on 5-year Treasury bonds, which actually went down during the worst of the crisis. The other is the rate on "high yield" corporate bonds, the bonds of companies considered more risky than average by the markets. Not only did the rates these companies had to pay soar after the crash but as noted above the number of companies falling into this classification increased 50 times over.

We must re-flate the currency, the government said. But it had already done so—within the Green Zone. In the Green Zone, money was cheap and freely available for anyone up for a shopping spree down those mean streets where assets were priced in hard-to-get deflated dollars. But the people of the Green Zone, the best of whom are careful to a fault, and the worst of whom had spent years making an easy living as grifters, frauds, and crony capitalists, don't like it on the mean streets. No matter how tempting the bargains or how cheaply they could borrow the money to buy, they would rather not venture out.

The ugliest possible end to such a panic is that prices in the Red Zone—General Growth Properties worth $10 billion, not $30 billion—actually become right. The real economic value of GGP and other assets like it permanently falls by two-thirds. The economy contracts so badly that GGP's rental income contracts from $2 billion to less than $700 million. At that point GGP is "really" worth only $10 billion, even with interest rates of 5 percent. Once that happens interest rates can go back down to 5 percent. Green Zone interest rates and Red Zone interest rates can reach equilibrium but only because so much value in the Red Zone has been destroyed.

This is, roughly speaking, the Great Depression scenario. A credit collapse destroys the real economy. We did not (knock on wood) get quite there. But the credit collapse of 2008 did cause an enormous amount of real permanent economic damage.

How could it have been prevented? We think, as we wrote at the time, that the solution was almost embarrassingly simple.

Remember, the core problem was that interest rates in the

government Green Zone were low because no one believed that the government, or those under its immediate protection, could go broke, while rates in the real economy Red Zone were super high, because there was terror abroad.

The obvious solution was to close the spread between those two interest rates by direct action in corporate bond markets. If a panic in credit markets has pushed the spread between government and private interest rates destructively high, and the only buyer able to face down the panic is the government, then the government should attack the panic, and thus the spread, directly. Sell Treasuries and buy any corporate bond in sight that appears to be priced at a large discount to its economic value, starting with the best bargains. Had the government done this the week Lehman fell, the crisis would have been over in days.

The $700 billion TARP bailout of the banks, put in place on October 3, 2008, was inefficient even in its original form because it was focused on buying the worst paper off the balance sheets of the most endangered institutions rather than buying the good but ridiculously cheap paper in the open market. TARP was focused on propping up crooked institutions, not calming the market panic threatening the entire economy. The government acted as if the problem was the collapsing price of bad bonds held by money-center banks. That was true a year earlier. After September 15, the real problem was the collapsing price of good bonds held by everyone else.

Still, it might have worked, almost inadvertently, because at least the government was planning to buy some paper from someone. But the next step, the October 14 "fix" of TARP to make it look more like what the Europeans (those economic geniuses) were doing by investing directly in the banks made it much worse. That was the moment the government really established the Green Zone and institutionalized crony capitalism.

What was needed, instead of TARP, was a three-sentence piece of legislation: (1) For the next one hundred eighty days the U.S. Treasury is authorized to buy asset-backed securities whose price appears to be an extreme discount from economic value. (2) For the purposes of calculating the debt of the United States, securities purchased under this authorization shall be credited against that debt at purchase price. [This to eliminate the need for an appropriation, allowing Congress to stay under the radar where it likes to be.] (3) All securities acquired under this authorization must be sold within twenty-four months.

What was needed was for the government (the only buyer that could safely venture into the Red Zone to exercise real capitalist judgment about value) to lead the market, not follow it down; to pursue profit, not subsidize failure. Instead, the same government that was massively subsidizing corrupt banks turned its back on firms that were in trouble only because of the government's fecklessness. The demon of moral hazard and the specter of socialism were duly invoked to excuse leaving victims of the government's collateral damage to die in the streets. Meanwhile the terrorists, who had done the government's will by expanding home ownership, underwriting government debt, and in numberless other ways, were re-funded to fight another day.

We accept that the government had to intervene with the banks. We thought it should have been done a year before. But the idea that saving markets and supporting good bonds is somehow more socialist than shipping public money to bad banks, as was frequently implied by the Bush administration's self-styled champions of capitalism, is exactly backwards. What was needed was for the only viable investor at the time, the government, to behave in a ruthless capitalist fashion.

The single most powerful advantage in a market panic is to have information most investors lack. In such a panic, the most informed potential investor is always the government. The government has three unique advantages:

The government has privileged access to the books of troubled firms.

The government cannot be caught in a liquidity squeeze, where being "right" doesn't matter because you don't have the cash to maintain a position against a market tsunami. All other investors, no matter how large, are ultimately subject to liquidity worries. Only the investor that can print its own money is immune.

Finally, the government knows (one hopes) what it, the government, is going to do. The unpredictability of government behavior—political risk—is a huge burden on investors in a crisis. That unpredictability had already been devastating. Only the government is immune.

With those advantages, the government should be able to restore market function by making open bids in public markets for severely underpriced assets and do it profitably. And as long as the government doesn't lose money by doing this it creates neither a subsidy nor a moral hazard. In September 2008, with no buyers to be found for trillions in securities, almost any bid would have bought the government a bargain and helped stabilize markets.

The Constitution of the United States charges the government with issuing money and regulating its value. In a modern economy, the government does that through credit markets. When, because of a general collapse of trust, the government becomes the only entity capable of sustaining credit markets, to do so is neither socialism nor a subsidy for folly. It is a minimally required regulatory function. Sustaining the credit markets that sustain the dollar is, in principle, indistinguishable from the government sustaining the dollar by accepting dollars in payment of taxes, or in olden days, presenting a bearer of dollars with gold on demand.

If a government will not make a market in its own currency, who will? In a modern economy, credit markets are the government's currency. To allow them to disappear is to allow its own currency to disappear, which is more or less what happened. Bonds sold for pennies on the dollar because as credit markets collapsed dollars became catastrophically scarce and costly. As dollars soared in price, all other financial instruments crashed.

Markets run on information and on trust. As a matter of law, the government has access to abundant information that private investors are, as a matter of law, denied. When trust breaks down and information becomes as scarce as dollars, it is the duty of the government, which makes the rules that govern the flow of information and establish trust in markets, to re-establish both. Closed-door deals spiriting public money into rotten banks do neither.

CHAPTER SEVENTEEN

Crony Capitalism in Crisis

W hy was the crash so severe, so much more damaging than the 1987 or 1998 crises, or even the tech wreck? In the weeks and months after the crash, the most popular answer we heard was that, finally, this time, for real, the nation, which had been borrowing far too much money for far too long, was truly "deleveraging," cutting back on debt. In those previous crises though individual sectors may have deleveraged, the debt merely moved around. The gas escaping from one bubble simply inflated another. Tech money became housing money. We had never really faced the music, so this story goes. Now, finally, we were.

This was clearly untrue. From the seizure of Fannie and Freddie onward, debt had been piling up at an astonishing rate. The only thing that changed with the crash was who was allowed to borrow. Under the new regime it was only the government and its friends.

Consider one rather bizarre phenomenon that occurred after the crash. Remember credit default swaps? In case you don't, a credit default swap, or CDS, is an insurance policy for a bond. The buyer of a swap pays an insurance premium to the seller. If the bond never defaults, the seller gets to keep the premiums and makes money. If the bond defaults, however, the seller must make good the losses suffered by the buyer of the policy.[97]

Swaps have a legitimate purpose. Bond owners, for instance, may buy CDS to hedge away the risk of default. But they can be abused as they were, for instance, by AIG, the huge insurance firm that went broke in September of 2008. AIG collapsed in large part because it had issued swaps (insurance policies) without having enough capital to pay out the damages if the covered bonds defaulted.

Issuing a CDS contract, selling insurance on a bond, is a lot like buying the bond itself. The issuer of a CDS contract, just like the buyer of a bond, makes money if the bond performs. By contrast, buying a CDS contract, buying insurance on a bond, is a lot like going short on a bond. Both the short seller and the insurance buyer make money if the bond does badly. So bond prices and the prices of CDS contracts should move in proportion to each other.

Bizarrely, for much of the fall of 2008, that was not happening. Prices reversed. Bonds were relatively cheaper than they should have been compared to CDS prices, which were relatively higher. This should have been impossible. Not only should the prices of the bond and the insurance contract ordinarily be equivalent, but given the collapse of AIG and the woes of other firms that had issued CDS contracts without adequate backing, if anything, the CDS contracts should have been cheaper than the bonds. CDS contracts were in disrepute, if not quite as "toxic" as mortgage-backed securities. And given the trouble the issuing companies were in, we should have been seeing mass sell-offs of the contracts as AIG and others tried to raise cash.

This was especially true because the GOOD PEOPLE who bought CDS insurance against a credit collapse, like, oh, the great hedge fund manager John Paulson, who made billions shorting mortgages, and our own beloved Whitebox, were much less leveraged and had borrowed much less money than the BAD PEOPLE like AIG who sold insurance against a credit collapse without having the money to pay up if it happened. In a general deleveraging, one would expect the BAD PEOPLE who issued the contracts to be forced to sell out their positions cheaply as they lost their credit lines. But the GOOD PEOPLE who had borrowed less to begin with should have been able to hold on to their investments. So bonds should have kept their value as CDS contracts lost theirs.

Why did the opposite happen? Simple, the government, in good crony-capitalist fashion, had its fingers on the scale. The government, through its pet banks, was pulling credit from bond owners, like hedge funds, forcing them to sell, undercutting bond prices. But the naked issuers of CDS contracts, like AIG, were sitting pretty in the Green Zone, with plenty of government money. Yes, AIG did unwind CDS contracts over time, but in a much more leisurely fashion than it would have done without the government's support. Meanwhile, bond owners were being forced to sell at panic prices. In effect the government was subsidizing CDS contracts written by crooks and penalizing bonds of crucial American companies bought by honest investors.

In the first days after the crash, the handful of big banks that serve as "prime brokers" to hedge funds, extending us the short-term credit we need to buy and sell securities, began to cut back on that lending, or at least warn us they might. That was hardly a surprise. In a bank panic firms become less willing to lend.

Then the government launched TARP, pumping hundreds of billions into the banks and effectively assuming control. The explicitly stated purpose of this program was to get the banks to resume lending, reviving credit markets. It did not happen. The banks saved by TARP, the banks that were shouting "how high" every time Hank Paulson said "jump," responded to the government's largesse by tightening credit—dramatically. We and every sound hedge fund we know of found it much tougher to borrow after the TARP program than before.

Hedge funds, if not the largest holders of corporate bonds, are certainly the crucial market makers: they do most of the buying and selling. When the government's pet banks took away hedge fund financing, they guaranteed bond prices would stay in free fall. For months, almost the only buyers of corporate bonds were the companies that had originally issued the bonds, seeing an opportunity to retire their own debt at dimes on the dollar. Nearly everyone else in the Red Zone was being forced to sell.

Fortunately most hedge funds are far less leveraged than popularly believed, and certainly less leveraged than the huge banks that are regulated by the Federal Reserve, the SEC, and the FDIC, but were often leveraged twenty or thirty to one. In 2004 the relevant congressional committee received with greatest equanimity the assertion that Fannie and Freddie were *underleveraged* because they had only borrowed $30 for every $1 of capital, and they really should be borrowing $50.

Leverage on that scale is almost unheard of among hedge funds for the simple reason that the people who lend us money (that would be those hugely leveraged regulated banks) wouldn't stand for it. Well, that is not the only reason. Also most hedge funds are run by people who are: smarter than people who work at banks; principal investors in their own funds with their own fortunes at risk; and acutely aware that they are not "too big to fail" and cannot expect to be rescued by the government if they behave stupidly.

And that's why CDS contracts were worth far more than their referenced bonds. It was not AIG—or Citi or Merrill—being forced to liquidate, but Citadel and dozens of other hedge funds. AIG and Citi and Merrill all got to hold on to their positions because they were being backed by the government, or in Merrill's case, because Bank of America is backed by the government. Meanwhile, the government's pet banks were putting margin calls on hedge funds.

The rhetoric of the Bush administration, before and during the crisis, was all that any real capitalist could wish. But the rhetoric was employed by an administration whose institutional dishonesty made the pathological but personal lies of Richard Nixon or Bill Clinton look like plain dealing.

Persistently the government played the part of the bold but honest sheriff who might have to shoot some bad guys but would ultimately save the town, or at least the market. And consistently it did just the opposite. It selectively protected institutions that deserved to die while firing Katyushas into the civilian population. This was a little hard to see at first not only because the rhetoric was so loud and so self-righteous, with those constant proclamations about how the bailouts must not create moral hazard, but also because at first glance it seemed as if the government *was* shooting the malefactors. But then why were they still standing?

Simple. It was not shooting them, it was merging with them. It was like *Invasion of the Body Snatchers*, with the government as the pods and the banks as their—whatever you call those things.

Henry Paulson, like Clinton's vastly admired secretary of the Treasury Robert Rubin, had been CEO of Goldman Sachs, the most prestigious and one of the most powerful investment banks in the world. Rubin then went on to become chairman of Citigroup. Noticing that, say, Goldman and Citi were treated rather more solicitously during the crisis then, say, Bear or Lehman, some commentators raised the question of conflicts of interest. Were the former Goldman guys protecting their own, to their own profit? Why did the government seem more intent on protecting the banks than the broader credit markets? Why did it give them all that money and then allow them to horde it, fat and happy in the Green Zone?

The notion of outright corruption always seemed silly to us. Instead, as the crisis progressed and fed upon the government's fecklessness, it occurred to us that we were seeing an even more powerful motive at work: The entirely natural and deeply human conviction that what is good for one's institutional friends is good for the country—the driving motive of crony-capitalist regimes everywhere.

We missed it at first. And in retrospect that is why, even though Andy had predicted the mortgage crunch, we really did not see the September crash coming. We did not grasp who we were messing with.

Contrary to the fevered rhetoric of the left, the Bush administration was not actually manned by idiots. It was, however, over-populated with personally successful, anti-intellectual, unreflective crony capitalists.

We have heard it said that crony capitalism is indistinguishable from socialism. Wrong. It's worse. No Democratic administration, with the exception of Roosevelt's first term, has been as abusive of financial markets as the Bush administration. The single point that most distinguishes Roosevelt's first disastrous term from the rest of his merely ineffective reign was that in the first term Roosevelt ran economic policy personally. Later he got bored and turned it over to the intellectuals. These were the sincere socialists, who—awful as they were—were an amazing improvement over Roosevelt personally dictating the day's gold price over breakfast (in bed as Amity Shlaes relates!), or pursuing his latest vendetta against industrialist dissenters from his agenda.

Like most people, socialists have the virtues of their vices. Socialism's great weakness is its tendency to excessive abstraction, to thinking in terms of classes rather than individual cases, to excessive awe for impersonal macro-economic forces like History, or Aggregate Demand, and too little respect for the work of men. In this the socialists are not unlike the professors who worship at the altars of inhumanly efficient markets.

This weakness comes with it own strengths. The socialists are an intellectual party comfortable with abstraction and with theory. Moreover, precisely because they have visionary and ambitious goals, at least since Lenin and his New Economic Policy the socialists have recognized they can get where they want to go only by riding on the back of capitalism.

Crony capitalists have neither the inclination for theory nor the interest in general economic success that attaches to the socialists. It is no accident that in our lifetime all the worst administrations for economic policy have been Republican any more than it is an accident that the single best was also Republican. From its very founding, there have been two factions in the GOP, the strong-ownership, free-market capitalist faction (Lincoln, Coolidge, Reagan) and the crony-capitalist faction (Grant, TR, Hoover, Nixon, the Bushes), which prefers weak owners who make dependable allies of government. Nor should it surprise that the most successful Republican administration of the twentieth century was led by a former Democrat, instinctively comfortable with broad visions and high ideals. Reagan was so comfortable with theory—and principle—that his critics faulted him for his tendency to see the world in sharp contrasts of black and white, right and wrong, ignoring as they said, the more subtle shades of gray distinguished by the sophisticates.

No one is more sophisticated than the crony capitalist, to

whom everything is gray and no man is a greater fool than the man of principle. The crony capitalists pride themselves on their grim realism, on being unburdened by ideas, on their infinite flexibility and pragmatism. All of which comes down to you can't trust them as far as you can throw them.

Unlike the socialists, the crony capitalists do not depend upon the general success of the economy to achieve their larger goals. For one thing, they can hardly be said to have larger goals. The crony capitalist is instinctively satisfied with the notion of a zero-sum game, which, for his purposes, is better than a rising tide that lifts all boats. What good is it to the crony capitalist to see all boats lifted? Will *all* boats remember the favor?

Crony capitalism is widely identified with the personal corruption that everywhere ultimately attends it. This is a mistake. The crony-capitalist politician is often not corrupt in the ordinary sense. What did Hank Paulson gain personally from bullying financial markets to the brink of a general economic collapse?

At its heart crony capitalism consists in a deep skepticism about the efficacy of ideas, the practicality of principle. Or at least it is a deep skepticism in the breast of the rare crony capitalist contemplative enough to achieve such a highly intellectual state. For most of them, it is not so much that they are skeptical of the power of ideas but that the notion of such power has never occurred to them. They are the Republican version of rebels without a cause, conformists without a clue.

Teddy Roosevelt is a stellar example. TR was not personally corrupt. And his admirers rarely think of the great trust-buster as "pro-business." He lands in the crony-capitalist category because he was a man both egotistical and anti-intellectual (socialists being egotistical and intellectual) who approached economic policy as a personal struggle between the righteous and the wicked, with righteousness defined as being on the same side as TR. TR's rhetoric was idealistic, but it was the idealism of Narcissus. The war against the trusts was a deeply personal campaign foreshadowing his cousin's vendetta against the "malefactors of great wealth" a generation later.

Lincoln, rarely considered a capitalist icon, did more for strong and able ownership than any president in U.S. history, perhaps more than any leader in world history. He sold millions of acres of land held by a neglectful government, transfering ownership into the hands of new owners who would make a garden in the wilderness. He transferred ownership of millions of men from masters who abused their own property back to the men themselves, the best owners of all.

For a long time the common but misleading association of crony capitalism with personal corruption did actually keep us from understanding the Bushies. We were impatient, for instance, with the usual absurd leftist fantasies about how we went to war in Iraq so Haliburton could bill for the rebuild. Dismissing the absurdity, we missed the reality behind it. Fevered as were the left's visions of Cheney as grand high mugwump of the military industrial complex, there was a hint very soon after the invasion of what the Bushies were really about. At that time, Jack Kemp did a piece for the *Wall Street Journal*, making the ingenious but obviously correct suggestion about what should be done with Iraq's oil revenues. Create one or several Iraqi petroleum firms and distribute the shares of each equally to every Iraqi citizen. This would have brought multiple benefits, including increasing the incentives for unity and civil peace. Most of all, it would have given capital to the citizens, whose wishes, roughly organized through markets, could then establish the priorities for reconstruction.

It was perhaps the best idea any public figure proposed in the course of the war. It never had a chance with the Bush administration. (The Democrats never took it up, it being no part of the socialist program to give property to actual people.) It never had a chance not because Dick Cheney contemplated a rake-off from the Haliburton contracts but because Cheney, Bush, and the rest knew Haliburton et al., and they didn't know Iraqi citizens. Crony capitalists are always statists, not in theory, like the socialists, but in practice, because they cannot let go of the impulse to control events. Controlling events means staying within the narrow boundaries of their experience and imagination, not to mention their Rolodexes. Iraq needs to be rebuilt? Call in the certified, pedigreed, well-connected, quasi-official rebuilders. The Democrats would do the same thing in their place (with bigger minority set-asides) and tell themselves they were doing it for the people. The crony capitalist does it because he wants nothing to do with the people.

This was precisely the mistake Paulson made with TARP (and the reason congressional Democrats mostly supported TARP and Republicans of the free-market-capitalist faction mostly opposed it). Even in the original version, TARP was conceived as a plan to save institutions, not restore order to markets. Even back when the plan was to buy bonds, not banks, the bonds to be bought were the worst paper on the balance sheets of the worst biggest banks. It apparently never occurred to Treasury to go into the open market and buy the most deeply discounted sound bonds to stem the general panic.

The open market solution did not occur to them because it never would occur to a crony-capitalist regime. It would amount to giving money to people unknown to the regime. Never mind that these payments would not have been gifts or subsidies for the simple reason that the government would have been making great deals. A crony-capitalist government will always favor subsidizing knaves and fools it knows and believes it can control, to letting capital and power slip away to those whose only claim is that they know what to do with it. The crony capitalist is too smart to be fooled by that. Like the wicked steward of the parable, like all the children of the serpent, he is sure it's not what you know but who you know that matters in this world.

The Keynesians try to conjure up prosperity by pumping up an abstraction called aggregate demand, forcing dollars into the economy. The crony capitalists try to do it with "targeted" tax cuts and "industrial policy" subsidizing favored firms. Reagan launched and Clinton sustained the greatest boom in American history by allowing investors and entrepreneurs to keep their own money and profit from their own judgments.

One incomprehensible Bush behavior after another becomes all too easy to understand once one grasps who they really were. We never imagined that only weeks after Treasury had urged investors to pump their capital into Fannie and Freddie it would then incinerate those same investors. We did not imagine it because we were thinking about the Bush administration as "not stupid." And they were not stupid. Right answer, wrong question.

From the framing "not stupid" it made no sense to toast Fannie's and Freddie's investors. From the framing "crony capitalists," it made perfect sense. Fannie and Freddie are liberal Democrat institutions, their dislike of which the Bush administration never troubled to conceal. As for the investors, a large percentage of them were community banks, a group that cut no ice with a straight-from-Wall-Street Treasury Department. A significant minority were hedge funds. And the Wall Street banks hate hedge funds with the special intensity that only a poseur feels for the real thing. As for the disincentive effects of teaching investors that the government sees nothing wrong with luring investors into the open only to shoot them, well, that is a rather abstract thought.

CHAPTER EIGHTEEN

Capitalism Without Capitalists

Capitalists are owners. Capitalism rests on strong ownership.

Being an owner means more than having the right to the income from an asset. Ownership implies both the legal right and the practical capacity to make judgments about the care and use of the asset. Judgment and ownership are inseparable. Both the mortgage crisis and the crash are best understood as the result of government policies that pushed trillions of dollars in assets out of the hands of relatively strong owners and into the hands of weak owners.

The slide into weak ownership that precipitated the mortgage crisis may be seen first in the mortgages themselves. A homeowner with a traditional 30-year, fixed-rate mortgage, carrying a payment that he can well afford, and substantial equity in the house is almost as strong an owner as the fellow with no mortgage at all. A man with a zero down payment, adjustable-rate mortgage, paying a low teaser rate, and hoping to flip the house in a rising market is hardly an owner at all. His fate depends not primarily on his own diligence and discipline but on outside forces and unknowable "information" about the future.[98] The term for someone who rests his economic fate on unknowable future events is not "owner," or even "investor," but "speculator."

The new-style bank or mortgage originator planning to sell off the mortgage as soon as possible similarly is hardly an owner at all compared to a bank or savings and loan that retains the mortgages it makes.

The ultimate investors who bought shares in the mortgage pools? Weak as well. In chapter nine we remarked on the weakness of public shareholders. Yet even a shareholder in a pubic company is more an owner than an investor in a structured mortgage pool. Based on the regular financial reports and other disclosures public companies are required to make, a diligent shareholder may be able to glean some sense of where a company is headed and decide whether he wants to go along for the ride. The investor in a "structured" mortgage-backed security knows far less than any diligent shareholder of a public company.

Public companies have senior managers, chosen by the board, with fairly clear legal authority and access to information. In the mortgage debacle ultimately there was not even a manager class. The nation's great banks, which largely funded the mortgage market, lacked even the cloudy information corporate managers normally depend on. That's how Morgan Stanley's sophisticated algorithms could persuade the banks' officers it had less than $100 million at risk only weeks before it would begin write-downs of many billions.

Then, of course, there is the government, the biggest player and the weakest owner of all.

Fannie and Freddie controlled something like half the U.S. mortgage market, dwarfing all other players. They shared the problems of the great banks in not really knowing what they owned or the risks they were running. But they had an even worse problem: figuring out who was in charge. Each had a board, with both government and shareholder-elected members. But the boards could hardly be said to be in charge when the firms' lifeblood was political support from Congress.

On the other hand Congress does not run things either. Congress is a committee. So who does?

If on Monday the secretary of the Treasury tells the twins their mission is to preserve the nation's capital, and then on Tuesday the chairman of the relevant House committee tells them affordable housing comes first, and the Fed, which owns so much of their paper, proposes a course correction on Wednesday, and the president on Thursday says their job is hope and change, what does that mean?

In the wake of the crash, ambiguities of ownership have only gotten worse. Who, today, owns the banks, or GM, or AIG? Who supervises management, rewards good performance, punishes bad, settles compensation? Congress? Or one congressman with a microphone? The president? The president before the bonus scandal broke, or after?

Who has skin in the game? The taxpayers, to be sure. But they are the weakest owners of all. Taxpayers make public shareholders look omnipotent.

The problem of government management is not that taxpayers are dumber than shareholders nor even that government bureaucrats are less able than private managers. There is no reason to suppose either of those things is true. The problem is that political control renders ownership even more ambiguous than in a widely held public company.

The good thing about public financial markets is that they can assemble very large amounts of capital swiftly. The speed and efficiency with which they do this can sometimes compensate for the shortcomings of weak ownership. During the crisis, the U.S. Treasury began to replace public financial markets because it seemed impossible to otherwise raise capital on the scale that appeared necessary. Intruding the political sector into the process of funding public companies makes everything that is already bad about public companies even worse. Public companies raise billions voluntarily from strangers to finance an enterprise whereof these investors know little and have only the weakest control over management. Today the government raises trillions involuntarily from taxpayers to fund enterprises without any identifiable management at all.

The driving force behind this massive shift from strong ownership to weak ownership was the ideology of modern finance. Replacing the notion of free markets as an essential context for capitalist creativity was the worship of supposedly efficient markets as substitutes for capitalists themselves.

Many times in our professional lives we have heard colleagues say things like, "I am a capitalist, even though I acknowledge that markets are not perfectly efficient." This gets the matter exactly backwards. The truth is the world needs capitalists because markets can never be perfectly efficient. Systems are essential to civilization. They stand for the thinking that has already been done. But they cannot replace the next thought or judgment that needs to be made.

Far from being a truly capitalist idea, the notion of efficient markets is more nearly socialist because it is essentially materialist.

In the 1930s, George Orwell, himself a dedicated socialist, puzzled over why socialism seemed so unappealing, especially to much of the English working class, even those leading the most brutal lives such as the miners. He concluded that people identified socialism with "efficiency," which the socialists were always talking about. People didn't like that because this "efficiency" seemed inhuman. Socialism was the welfare lady criticizing the miners' wives because their homes were untidy or because they spent too much money on tea and sugar and too little on vegetables. Socialist art depicted a spotlessly clean glass-and-steel world full of heroic workers—and real workers were repulsed. Perhaps they did not want to work heroically. (Goodness knows we don't.) Perhaps they wanted to spend more time at the pub. (We'll be there!)

In those naïve days the socialists' favorite charge against capitalism was inefficiency. Both the poverty of the workers and the wealth of the owners were believed to be the result of the massive waste implicit in private ownership and the brutality of private prejudice empowered by that ownership. The poor were oppressed precisely because the system was too human, too dependent on private judgments too often made badly. Collectives and committees would sort things out. Private judgment would be replaced by public systems, perfectly informed, consistently rational, faultlessly allocating resources including not only the money but the labor of men, yielding unheard of prosperity shared rationally among all.

Perhaps because the equation of socialism and efficiency now strikes most people as comic at best, we have tended to forget this little history of ideas. And, of course, the sort of people who go around talking about the perfect efficiency of markets seem anything but socialists. Yet, at bottom, the dream of market efficiency and the dream of socialist efficiency are the same dream. Each dreams of dispensing with human foibles and prejudice, with human error—but also human judgment—and replacing them with a vast central calculator "fully accounting for" all available information so as to make efficient economic decisions.

True, in most versions of the socialist dream, the calculator is made of committees and commissars, measuring and meeting, explicitly trying to determine the best for all. In the efficient market dream no one runs the calculator. But in spirit this difference is less than it seems. A good deal of early socialist literature imagined that the central planning would actually be done by an astonishingly efficient and all-knowing computer, which is really how efficient market folks think of the New York Stock Exchange. These days the computers actually exist.

At heart, both yearn for capitalism without capitalists.

Modern portfolio theory is materialism applied to investment, as if Marx had gone to Harvard Business School and then worked at Goldman Sachs rather than hanging out with Engels and writing incomprehensible books.

Adam Smith did a great thing by carefully delineating how markets function, giving us profound insights into the dangers and unintended consequences of meddling with them. But markets are only half the capitalist story. Markets exist in all societies, capitalist or not. Markets are simply one system of accountability for the allocators of capital. Every society needs such systems of accountability and capitalist democracies use several. In addition to market accountability, there is political accountability: Call your city councilman; get a pothole fixed. There is bureaucratic accountability: Go down to the bureau of potholes; fill out the appropriate form; the bureaucrats determine whether your pothole meets the standards for fixing.

Various systems of accountability are best suited to different situations: even most capitalist societies leave the streets and other common goods to the bureaucrats and politicians.

None of the various systems of accountability, however, produce anything themselves. They simply reward or punish, more or less efficiently, those who, given charge of some capital, use it for better or worse. The overwhelming evidence of experience is that free economic markets are especially good at rewarding the creative and productive use of capital. This is an extremely powerful and important truth. Yet no matter how free the market, it is the men not the market who do the creating. It is the mental, physical, and moral efforts of men liberated by the market who, as co-creators with the good God, make the good things of this world. Free markets are important primarily because of whom they set free. Once we begin to imagine that it is the market that does the making, or the thinking, we are lost.

The source of all new wealth, all the value in a product that cannot be reduced to its accountable costs, is right judgment in the presence of uncertainty. Such judgments, such resolutions of uncertainty into productive knowledge rarely take the form of a momentary brilliant inspiration. They more commonly issue from an arduous and disciplined course of trial and error, as the lives of the great entrepreneurs tell us.

The reward of right judgment, the new wealth created by the entrepreneur, is called profit. The worshippers of efficient markets believe that the market of perfect competition, the market of perfect knowledge, the market in which the judgment of the entrepreneur is irrelevant, the market of no profit has actually come to earth in the form of modern securities markets.

This apparently capitalist affirmation denies the very possibility of the central capitalist act, the heart of the capitalist drama. To claim that any actual existing market makes human judgment irrelevant is to deny the role of entrepreneurial commitment and creativity, diligence and judgment in creating wealth. If all the value in a product, or an investment, can be perfectly equated with its accustomed costs, if the sum is never more than its parts, if the best any investor can do is to passively give the all-perfect market his money and be paid the market-determined return, then the old left-wing complaint that capitalism is just the rich getting richer is vindicated. Like all materialist notions, this one is essentially determinist. Every future distribution of wealth is perfectly predicted by any past distribution because every person's income is a linear function of his prior bank balance. Who wouldn't take up the red flag if that were true?

Materialism and determinism, as Marx well understood, destroy the morality of capitalism. Entrepreneurship is not only the creative force of capitalism, it is the moral test of capitalism. Only if the efforts of the entrepreneur can be fruitful, only if future states of wealth can be altered by the superior judgment, skill, and moral commitment of the entrepreneur, only if the "old-fashioned way" to make money really is to earn it does capitalism have a moral basis.

Once we grasp the morality of entrepreneurship, the morality of creation, then we are able to see it in its humbler forms throughout the economy. Once we see that the essence of entrepreneurship is to overthrow determinism, to alter the economic fates, often in large ways, then we can see that it is not only entrepreneurs who can do this. Any diligent worker or careful saver can do the same. Like the entrepreneur, the diligent worker and careful saver give the lie to the materialist and determinist worldview. They can alter fate because they make free, which is to say, moral choices to be thrifty or hardworking or productive in a system that rewards such behavior. Societies that reward such behaviors, and, above all, societies that commend them morally, societies that call the thrifty and hardworking good and deserving, prosper. Societies that deny the moral causes of wealth grow poor and turn to war and persecution. They usually end up killing the Jews.

If the crisis had its roots in an ideology of finance that derided judgment, denied the entrepreneur, and weakened ownership, it found its consummation in the tendency of crony-capitalist regimes, left and right alike, to encourage and exploit such weakness. Having profited politically for decades from undermining homeownership under the guise of extending it, the government diverted attention from the moral causes of the crisis. It first shielded the guilty, then actively rewarded them, and finally punished the virtuous. It was this moral failure that turned a credit crunch into the most dangerous and damaging economic crisis since the Great Depression and even now threatens to extend the damage out for years to come.

ENDNOTES

1   The "spread" is the difference between two interest rates, usually the rate on Treasury bills vs. the rate of some other category of bond. In this case the other category was "high yield" bonds, a.k.a. "junk."

2   Estimates vary.

3   We are making these numbers up.

4   We are ignoring amortization to keep from driving our readers to their calculators, or worse.

5   Buy it with borrowed money.

6   International Monetary Fund, *The Influence of Credit Derivative and Structured Credit Markets on Financial Stability*, March 2006, Report 2, 51–80.

7   Ibid.

8   Henry A. Davis, "The Definition of Structured Finance, Results from a Survey," *Journal of Structured Finance* 2, no. 3 (Fall 2005): 5–10.

9   Matt Hudgins, "Why CDOs Are Hot," *National Real Estate Investor* (June 1, 2006), www.nreionline.com.

10 International Monetary Fund, *The Influence of Credit Derivative and Structured Credit Markets on Financial Stability*, March 2006, Report 2, 51–80.

11 Ibid.

12 Ibid.

13 Ibid.

14 Frank J. Fabozzi, "The Structured Finance Market: An Investor's Perspective," *Financial Analysts Journal* 61, no. 3 (May/June 2005): 27–40.

15 Ibid.

16 Ibid.

17 The same risk can be systemic in relation to smaller sets and idiosyncratic in relation to larger sets. If the NYSE drops while my diversified global portfolio remains stable, the NYSE movement is idiosyncratic with respect to the global portfolio because it can be presumed that the driving factor is specific to the NYSE or American markets.

18 Conversation with Carver Mead. We have paraphrased and probably butchered his actual remarks.

19 Unlike the owner of an ETF, or "exchange-traded fund," the trader of an index does not actually own the underlying stocks, which is why we call it a "pure bet."

20 As we discuss in chapter nine, there are stabilizing factors especially for large, well-established commodity markets. The common denominator in the stabilizing factors is that they consist of current knowledge that blunts the impact of future information, e.g., the weather. The existence of irrigation systems is one example of such existing knowledge. Because of irrigation we know that the crops will get some minimum of water regardless of drought. Grain elevators are another example: because we can store grains for years, the supply is not wholly dependent upon future information in the form of weather.

21 Richard A. Brealey, Stewart C. Myers, and Franklin Allen, *Principles of Corporate Finance* (NJ: McGraw-Hill, 2006): 192.

22 Robert C. Higgins, *Analysis for Financial Management*, 8th edition, (NJ: Irwin/McGraw-Hill, 2007), 52–53.

23 Frank K. Reilly and Keith C. Brown, *Investment Analysis and Portfolio Management*, 6th edition (South-Western College Publishing, 2002), 6.

24 David Paschal, "Risky Business, Big Rewards" [Entrepreneur's Notebook], *Nation's Business* 78, no. 3 (March 1990): 6.

25 http://thinkexist.com/quotes/victor_kiam/.

26 http://en.wikiquote.org/wiki/Ray_Kroc.

27 http://www.saidwhat.co.uk/quotes/favourite/thomas_j_watson/every_time_weve_moved_ahead_in_16686.

28 Karl D. Bays, "The Force of Entrepreneurship," *Business Horizons* 31, no. 1 (1988), remarks on the occasion of being recognized for "Distinguished Entrepreneurship" by the Wharton School of Business.

29 It would be unfair to Frank Hyneman Knight for us to attribute specific

bits and pieces of this chapter to his great work *Risk, Uncertainty and Profit*. But anyone who has had the great good fortune to read that book will see how great is our debt to it, even if we have adapted Knight's language and thought somewhat freely and to our own purposes.

30 Knight sharply distinguished risk and uncertainty in his technical language, but his special meaning for "risk" is not comprised in the ordinary use of the word.

31 Eugene Fama, "Efficient Capital Markets: A Review of Theory and Empirical Work," *Journal of Finance* 25, no. 2 (1970): 383.

32 Including the cost of risk. Thus stock market returns are not the result of entrepreneurial judgment but merely market-level compensation for a familiar cost.

33 Fama, 395.

34 Fama, 396.

35 Eugene Fama, "Efficient Capital Markets: II," *Journal of Finance* 46, no. 5 (December 1991): 1580.

36 Computers would have changed their minds.

37 See, for instance, Michael C. Jensen's "The Performance of Mutual Funds in the Period 1945–1964" in *The Journal of Finance* 23, no. 2 (May 1968): 389–416; and Jack L. Treynor's and Kay K. Mazuy's "Can Mutual Funds Outguess the Market" in *Harvard Business Review* (July/August 1966): 131–136.

38 Andrea Frazzini and Owen A. Lamont, "Dumb Money: Mutual Fund Flows and the Cross-Section of Stock Returns," NBER Working Paper No. W11526 (August 2005); available at SSRN: http://ssrn.com/abstract=776014.

39 International Monetary Fund, *The Influence of Credit Derivative and Structured Credit Markets on Financial Stability*, March 2006, Report 2, 51–80.

40 Some uncertainty would remain, in large part because of the volatility of public commodity markets, and, of course, our old friend—the weather!

41 Competitors do sometimes undersell at a loss for their own reasons, such as tight cash flow or in order to grab market share. But in theory, at least, the value thus obtained can be worked back into the equation to show that the underseller has not actually beaten the price. If this is not the case—if the underseller has actually created more value by selling below apparent cost—then he has had an entrepreneurial moment.

42 Smith was writing in the midst of an industrial revolution in which the cloth market did see very powerful innovation and dramatic improvement

in price and quality over time. And cloth markets can have booms, busts, and panics. Still, the general point holds.

43 Michael C. Jensen, "The Eclipse of the Public Corporation," *Harvard Business Review* (September/October 1989): 61–73. Jensen surveys research from a number of scholars, notably Stephen Kaplan.

44 Ibid.

45 Peter J Wallison, "The True Origins of This Financial Crisis," *The American Spectator*, February 2009.

46 Quoted in Stan J. Liebowitz's "Anatomy of a Train Wreck: Causes of the Mortgage Meltdown," a forthcoming chapter in *Housing America: Building Out of a Crisis*, Randall G. Holcombe and Benjamin Powell, eds. (NJ: Transaction Books, 2009), 8.

47 Liebowitz, 8.

48 Ibid.

49 Wallison, *The American Spectator*, February 2009.

50 Ibid.

51 Ibid.

52 Quoted in Stan J. Liebowitz's "Anatomy of a Train Wreck: Causes of the Mortgage Meltdown," Abstract, a forthcoming chapter in *Housing America: Building Out of a Crisis*, Randall G. Holcombe and Benjamin Powell, eds. (NJ: Transaction Books, 2009).

53 "Freddie Mac Pays Record $3.8 Million Fine," Associated Press, April 18, 2006; available at http://www.msnbc.msn.com/id/12373488/from/RSS/#storyContinued.

54 James R. Barth et al., *The Rise and Fall of the U.S. Mortgage and Credit Markets: A Comprehensive Analysis of the Meltdown* (NJ: John Wiley and Sons, 2009), 434.

55 Joe Nocera, "A Mission Goes Off Course," *New York Times*, August 23, 2008.

56 Wallison, *The American Spectator*, February 2009.

57 Peter J. Wallison and Charles W. Calomiris, "The Last Trillion-Dollar Commitment: The Destruction of Fannie Mae and Freddie Mac," *AEI Financial Services Outlook*; posted September 30, 2008.

58 Ibid.

59 Liebowitz, "Anatomy of a Train Wreck"

60 Ibid.

61 Steven Malanga, "Mortgage Deadbeats Plague Home Market," *Real Clear*

Markets, September 30, 2009.

62 "Eighth Periodic Mortgage Fraud Case Report to the Mortgage Bankers Association," Mortgage Asset Research Institute, April 2006.

63 Gretchen Morgenson, "Crisis Looms in Market for Mortgages," *New York Times,* March 11, 2007.

64 Unfortunately no comparable data are available for mortgage-backed securities prices from earlier periods.

65 The SEC imposed tougher mark-to-market rules in 2006. But the SEC had been pushing the industry toward mark-to-market since the early 1990s.

66 James R. Barth et al., *The Rise and Fall of the U.S. Mortgage and Credit Markets: A Comprehensive Analysis of the Meltdown* (NJ: John Wiley and Sons, 2009), 21.

67 Amherst Non-Agency Mortgage Market Monitor, Amherst Securities Group LP, reporting through September 2009.

68 Peter J. Wallison and Charles W. Calomiris, "The Last Trillion-Dollar Commitment: The Destruction of Fannie Mae and Freddie Mac," *AEI Financial Services Outlook*, posted September 30, 2008.

69 Zachary Goldfarb, "Affordable Housing Goals Scaled Back," *Washington Post*, September 24, 2008, quoted in "The Last Trillion-Dollar Commitment," by Wallison and Calomiris (see above).

70 Gretchen Morgenson, "Investors in Mortgage-Backed Securities Fail to React to Market Plunge," *New York Times* [*International Herald Tribune*], February 18, 2007.

71 Vikas Bajaj, "Global Sell Off: Freddie Mac Tightens Standards," *New York Times*, February 27, 2007.

72 Vikas Bajaj, "U.S. Urges Lenders to Revise Standards on Granting Credit," *New York Times*, March 3, 2007.

73 Greg Farrell, "Investors Cheer UBS, Citigroup Write-Downs," *USA Today*, October 2, 2007.

74 Citigroup press release, October 1, 2007.

75 "Citigroup's Day of Reckoning," CNNMoney.com, November 4, 2007.

76 Jonathan Stempel and Dan Wilchins, "Citigroup Axing Jobs, Dividend," Reuters in *Toronto Star*, January 17, 2008.

77 Fiona Walsh, "Citigroup To Shed 9,000 Jobs after Posting $5.1 Billion Loss," guardian.co.uk, April 18, 2008.

78 Greg Morcroft, "Merrill Swings To Loss on Huge Mortgage Hit," MarketWatch, October 24, 2007.

79   Bradley Keoun, "'Startling' $8 Billion Loss for Merrill Lynch," Bloomberg News in the *Seattle Times*, October 25, 2007.

80   Tim McLaughlin, "Merrill Lynch Takes About $16 Billion in Write-Downs," Reuters, January 17, 2008.

81   "Morgan Stanley Reports Record Third Quarter Results," Morgan Stanley press release, September 19, 2007.

82   David Ellis, "More Woes for Morgan Stanley," CNNMoney.com, December 20, 2007.

83   Quoted in Stan J. Liebowitz's "Anatomy of a Train Wreck: Causes of the Mortgage Meltdown," Abstract, a forthcoming chapter in *Housing America: Building Out of a Crisis*, Randall G. Holcombe and Benjamin Powell, eds. (NJ: Transaction Books, 2009).

84   F. William Engdahl, "The Financial Tsunami: SubPrime Mortgage Debt Is but the Tip of the Iceberg," globalresearch.ca, November 23, 2007.

85   Which does not mean, obviously, that the bank is supposed to be at risk for losing up to $100 million day after day. The idea is that if a big bad thing suddenly happens it will show up in the VaR number and the bank will take steps to reduce its risk quickly.

86   "Morgan Stanley Reports Record Results," Morgan Stanley press release, September 19, 2007.

87   David Enrich, "Citigroup Installs New Risk Managers," *Wall Street Journal*, February 28, 2008.

88   Mostly because the twins' bonds are longer-dated than T-bills and thus do carry some interest rate risk.

89   A quantitative description of "too big to fail" might help: say any firm employing assets exceeding $10 billion and leveraged more than five to one.

90   James R. Barth et al., *The Rise and Fall of the U.S. Mortgage and Credit Markets: A Comprehensive Analysis of the Meltdown* (NJ: John Wiley and Sons, 2009), 173.

91   Robert Novak, "Crony Image Dogs Paulson's Rescue Effort," *Chicago Sun-Times*, July 17, 2008.

92   Eric Dash, "U.S. Gives Banks Urgent Warning to Solve Crisis," *New York Times*, September 12, 2008.

93   Dash, *New York Times*, September 12, 2008.

94   Ibid.

95   Ibid.

96 To see this more clearly, remember that if the $30 billion in malls were refinanced at 15 percent, annual interest charges would have been $4.5 billion per year, more than double the total rental income. To get income back in line with expenses, the price of the malls—the amount financed—would have to come down to about $10 million so that interest cost would once again be less than rental income.

97 Actually the seller makes good the equivalent of the losses any holder of the bond would have sustained. He must pay these to the buyer of the policy regardless of whether the buyer ever actually held the bond.

98 This may not be entirely true if he is an expert "fixer upper" spinning dross into gold. But in such cases the owner has much more equity in the house, "sweat equity," than appears on his mortgage agreement.

ACKNOWLEDGMENTS

Most of the people who helped with this book will remain forever blissfully unaware of their responsibility: innumerable teachers, clients, colleagues, and friends who have contributed over many years to our education in the ways of markets. Any confusion or errors that remain are entirely their fault.

Among those whose aid was provided more consciously we must single out Marie Lavinio whose responsibility it is to take what Richard (laughably) considers a completed book and make it presentable to the world. Marie's rhythm section for *Panic* included Charles Bork on design and layout, who with his usual forbearance put the book through numerous rounds of corrections, and Nicole Muchmore and Lea Oksman on proof, whose diligence, it must be said, was a proximate cause of Charles's labors. (Charles bears them no ill will, we are sure.) Ann Salinger provided the index with her customary dispatch.

Long before Marie and her team got a book to work on, the manuscript got helpful reads from George Gilder, Maggie Gallagher, Lee Otis, and Susan Vigilante. George was encouraging, Maggie was kind, Lee was demanding, and Sue actually did some editing. Prof. Russell Hittinger provided important insight and recommended reading on the notion of judgment. If he is appalled by the mess we have made of it, he has only himself to blame for overestimating our ability to navigate the heights that his own intellect customarily inhabits.

Once we had a finished manuscript, as we thought, Louisa Gilder did an inspired edit, applying the 30 percent rule diligently and elegantly. If Louisa's edit provoked us to completely rewrite the book one more time, causing the copyright to commence in 2010 rather than 2009, well who's to say that's a bad thing.

Down the homestretch, our colleagues Scott Bettin and Moya Mulqueen helped with crucial research, and colleagues Paul Twitchell, Graham Cook, Rob Vogel, Jonathan Wood, and Mark Strefling provided useful comments. Richard would also like to thank Graham and colleague Nousha Magnusson for their forbearance during the last stages. We promise never to write another book, until the next one. And we would both like to thank Amy Borgstrom, as always, for her cheerful assistance.

Charles designed a cover based on an idea from Marie, which we both loved, but which the booksellers of the world regarded as excessively amusing for the gravity of the subject matter. Sam Torode stepped in, and, charged to muster all his own considerable gravitas, did the current splendid version. If you like being excessively amused go to www.capitalismbetrayed.com to see the original.

INDEX

Weber, M., 64
Whitebox, 11
"World portfolio," 30, 54

Yale School of Management, 107

Zero–sum games, 123